Under the Canopy

STORIES OF GOD'S ALL-ENCOMPASSING GRACE

CHARLES E. CRAVEY

In His Steps Publishing

Copyright © 2025 by Charles Edward Cravey

All rights reserved.

You may not reproduce any portion of this book in any form without written permission from the publisher or author, except as permitted by U.S. copyright law.

Revised Second Edition

All scripture is from the King James Version of the Holy Bible.

ISBN: 978-1-58535-050-6 (Paperback)

ISBN: 978-58535-052-0 (KINDLE EPUB)

Library of Congress Catalog Number: 2025905468

Contents

Foreword	VII
Dedication	IX
1. Chapter 1	1
2. A Primal Scream	3
3. Prophet of Doom	14
4. Quietly in the Night	25
5. "Repaint, Ye Thinners!"	35
6. Final Harvest	41
7. Familiar Things	48
8. Chapter 2	57
9. Under the Canopy	58
10. The Meaning of Our Lives	65
11. Things to Live By	73
12. Eye of the Beholder	80
13. Brush Strokes	88

14.	Excessive Happiness	94
15.	Learning the Hardest Lessons	102
16.	The Song Remembers When	112
17.	Justification	117
18.	I Saw God in the Muck and Mire	124
19.	Sheep and Shepherds	127
20.	Chapter 3	132
21.	The Maine Thing	133
22.	"Just Aren't Enough Rocks!"	140
23.	A Majestic Encounter	149
24.	The Master's Cut	154
25.	The First Day of the Rest of My Life	160
26.	Not Just a Cup of Coffee	165
27.	Pot-Liquor Hill	170
28.	Finding Greg Allman's Grave	175
29.	The Mighty Hiawassee	180
30.	One Square at a Time	182
31.	My Romance With Paper	188
32.	Grave Number 291	193
33.	Chapter 4	197

34.	Blackie's Arrival	199
35.	Butterfly Kisses	205
36.	The Legend of "Mr. Mac"	216
37.	The Night the Lights Went Out in Georgia	222
38.	What's My Destiny?	229
39.	Through the Eye of a Needle	234
40.	Carpe Diem	239
41.	Spiritual Growth in the Bahamas	243
42.	I Long to See You	247
43.	Driving at Night	252
44.	"I Just Came for the Barbeque!"	257
45.	Choosing a Life	263
46.	Chapter 5	265
47.	Diamonds in the Rough	267
48.	Sacrificial Love	271
49.	From Seattle With Love	275
50.	Budget Childcare	279
51.	Out of the Mouth of Babes	283
52.	In Closing	286
53.	Newspapers and Magazines	289

Foreword

Possessing an outstanding intellect and keen wit, Charles Cravey has used his superb writing skills in producing this book as a blessing to all who read and benefit from its profound insights. With a faithful, daily commitment to Jesus Christ, Charles has pastored churches effectively through the years and enhanced his talents through music and writing venues of all sorts. Charles is a multi-talented brother in Christ who has produced Christian works that have benefitted others across cultures.

With a contagious passion for Jesus Christ, his Lord, Charles has been creatively active in unique ways to proclaim the gospel visually and in other ways. Fact in point: Charles proclaimed the gospel standing on church roofs (e.g., Alamo UMC and Bloomfield UMC) to fulfill a pledge, "Fill the sanctuary with worshippers, and I will preach from this church's roof." Indeed, it was an impressive fulfillment of the admonition found in Matthew 10:22: "What I tell you in the dark, speak in the daylight; what is whispered in your ear, proclaim from the roofs" (NIV), "proclaim from the housetops" (TLB). I have the name "Charles Cravey" noted in the margin opposite this passage in my Bible.

I recommend this quality book for your reading and study. My gifted brother, Charles, has lived joyfully a lifetime of splendid dedication to Christ. Well done, Charles! Well done, good friend!

—The Rev. Dr. Hugh L. Davis, D. Min.

Perry, Georgia

June 2023

To God, I owe everything! He is "the way, the truth, and the life." (John 14:6).

To my dear wife, Renee, who has found fit to share her life with me for the past fifty-two years! Her teacher skills were much needed in editing this book, and she did it willingly. She also chose the title and suggested much-needed changes. Every man should have her as an asset. She has always been there for me! She gave birth to our two beautiful children, Jonathan and Angela, and they have both been a blessing.

Finally, to all those faithful, loving, and supportive church members, I have had the privilege of serving for the past fifty-two years. You have been wonderful, loving, and accepting.

Charles E. Cravey, March 2025

SHORT STORIES

One of the gifts of being a writer is that it gives you an excuse to do things, to go places and explore. Another is that writing motivates you to look closely at life, at life as it lurches by and tramps around.

—Anne Lamott, *Bird by Bird*

A Primal Scream

At her kitchen window, Clara Cramer stood cold and alone, staring at the flakes of snow falling aimlessly to the ground. Every fiber within her cried out for reason and an explanation of what had decidedly become the worst day of her life. Earlier that afternoon, Clara had laid her beloved husband, Sam, to rest in Christ Hill Cemetery, and now she was alone. At the close of the funeral service, Beatrice Carter had shared some disturbing news with Clara that shook her world. She stood there, as in a trance, trying to understand the circumstances of what she had just learned from Beatrice, when a lone dove flew into the window and fell to the ground. She watched as another dove came and landed beside the fallen one and then took flight again.

As Clara processed Beatrice's news, a mix of grief, confusion, and disbelief overwhelmed her. The winter landscape outside seemed to mirror the desolation she felt within. The sudden appearance of the doves felt like a poignant moment, a symbol of hope and companionship amid her solitude. Clara's heart ached for Sam, for the life they had shared, and for the uncertain future that now lay ahead of her.

The soft sound of the falling snow broke the quiet of the kitchen only and Clara's own ragged breaths. She knew she needed time to process everything that had happened, to come to terms with her new reality. But in that moment, as the doves took flight once more, Clara felt a glimmer of peace wash over her. It was a slight comfort, but amid her sorrow, it was enough to sustain her for the time being.

Clara's heart was as cold as stone as her mind speedily went through the motions of making sense out of what she had heard at the funeral. Deep within her psyche, a primal scream longed to be released, exposing her hurt and disappointment with Sam. The feeling was as if someone had strapped her to a cold metallic bed and given her a lethal dose of pentobarbital. The doctor could have easily pronounced her D.O.A. at 4:26 pm because she felt expired, undone. Sam, her beloved husband and best friend for the past 44 years, had died last week from a massive stroke. He had spent a rough week in the hospital, and they had done everything possible to save him, but ultimately to no avail. She would face innumerable medical fees and had only Sam's small retirement and social security from Sam's employment to survive on. Clara had never worked outside the home. Sam had wanted her to just concentrate on working at home and keeping things in order. They had a few cows, a few pigs, and a yard full of chickens that provided them meat and eggs all year round.

This sudden loss of her partner left Clara in a state of shock and uncertainty. The weight of grief and financial worries pressed down on her like a heavy burden. As she navigated the aftermath of Sam's passing, Clara grappled with a new reality, one where she would have to sustain herself without the support and companionship of her husband. The future seemed daunting and bleak, filled with challenges and unknowns.

Yet, amidst the darkness, Clara clung to the memories of her life with Sam, the love they shared, and the simple joys of their home and farm. In the quiet moments of solitude, she found solace in the familiar sights and sounds of their humble abode, a sanctuary that now held both cherished memories and profound loss. As Clara faced the daunting task of rebuilding her life without Sam by her side, she drew strength from the resilience and determination that had been the foundation of their enduring bond. The road ahead was uncertain, but Clara knew she would carry Sam's spirit with her, guiding her through the challenges that lay ahead.

Sam had dedicated 45 years of his life working at Cranston's Furniture store in downtown Swanson. The Cranston family held a deep appreciation for Sam's loyalty and devotion, and upon his retirement three years ago, they provided him with a generous severance package. Since then, Sam and Clara had been living a comfortable life, although they refrained from indulging in any luxuries.

Unfortunately, Sam's health declined, leading to a hospital stay filled with numerous tests, including a heart catheterization, brain scan, and neurological examinations. Throughout his ordeal, Clara, his devoted wife, never left his side. She spent each night in an uncomfortable chair by his hospital bed, only stepping away briefly for meals or restroom breaks. Clara's unwavering loyalty and love for Sam shone through as she supported him during his difficult time.

Marilyn, the adopted daughter of Sam and Clara, played a significant role in their lives. At 26 years old, she devoted hours to caring for her parents during their hospital stays, demonstrating her deep love and commitment to them.

Sam and Clara's journey to parenthood began when they learned about a child available for adoption at a local children's home. Sam, taking the lead, made all the arrangements for Marilyn's adoption when she was just nine months old. Despite their previous struggles with infertility, Clara and Sam felt blessed to have Marilyn in their lives.

Clara stayed at home to raise Marilyn, providing her with a nurturing environment and even homeschooling her until the eighth grade. Marilyn flourished under their care, becoming a well-rounded individual and a valuable help to Clara on their farm. Sam and Clara rejoiced at finally raising a child and were thankful for Marilyn in their lives.

Things around the farm had been great for the Cramer family. Clara, Sam, and Marilyn were the perfect match made in heaven. Townsfolk always talked about how happy they always seemed to be. Marilyn even began singing in the church choir and became a cheerleader on her high school cheer team. She was an exceptional child and never once got into trouble. Her graduating class chose her as Valedictorian. Clara and Sam were so overwhelmed.

After graduation, Marilyn married Billy Merritt. Billy was a provider and worked at the Stinson Elementary School as janitor. At night, Billy attended classes at the local university, where he eventually graduated with a master's degree in education. He then began teaching at the same school at which he had formerly worked. The teachers and staff loved Billy, and he leaped up the ranks until the School Superintendent eventually chose Billy to be principal at the same high school from which he had graduated!

Billy and Marilyn had two children, a beautiful daughter named Maria, and a son named Billy Joe, after his father. Their modest home was three miles from the Cramers in Stinson. They seemed the perfect couple, like Marilyn's adopted parents.

The funeral brought people out from several surrounding counties, including those who had known Sam through his work at the furniture store and from whom they had occasionally bought livestock. Sam was a well-respected individual known for his integrity and hard work, but some saw him as a dreamer, always chasing after unattainable goals like the man of La Mancha battling imaginary windmills. Clara, who lived with Sam, often noticed his tendency to dwell on the past, which occasionally troubled her. Despite this, she chose not to confront him about it, and they coexisted peacefully in their shared home.

Beatrice Carter, also known as Bea, was a well-known figure in the small town of Stinson. Her reputation as the town's busybody was well-earned, as she had a knack for uncovering and spreading the latest gossip. If there was something to know about someone in town, Bea was the one to ask. While her information was not always completely accurate, it was usually fairly close to the truth.

Bea's gossiping tendencies made her both a blessing and a curse to the residents of Stinson. Some appreciated her ability to keep them in the loop, while others found themselves the subject of her rumors and speculation. One day, Bea approached Clara at the cemetery with a surprising revelation about Marilyn's parentage. The news took aback Clara and questioned Bea's source of information.

The encounter between Bea and Clara underscored the power and impact of gossip in a small community like Stinson. Bea's insatiable curiosity and penchant for spreading rumors kept the town buzzing with speculation and intrigue. Love her or hate her. Beatrice Carter was the undisputed queen of gossip in Stinson.

"No, I didn't, Bea, and this is certainly not the time for your nonsense." Marilyn was already upset over losing Sam, and now the talk of the town was trying to give her some gossip. Who does she think she is? "I know, on good authority," Bea said, "that Marilyn is actually Sam's child." Sam and Rhonda Bassitt had an affair 26 years ago, and Rhonda became pregnant with Marilyn. Complications from childbirth later killed her, so they placed Marilyn in our local children's home for adoption because she had no family to claim her. The home agreed and assured Sam that they would keep their secret.

Not only did the news of Sam's affair break Clara's heart, but to know that their very daughter was Sam's. Really, Sam's!

Clara told Bea that it was not the time, nor the place, to be telling such lies, and that she would be in touch with her later. She would require facts and details about the entire story.

Now, as Clara stood in front of the kitchen window with the snow falling, she felt that someone had opened Pandora's Box and there was no way to return this information. Her heart grew colder and colder as the night approached.

Marilyn came by to check on her mom, Clara. However, Clara mentioned nothing about the rumor that was circulating. The rumor spread by old Beatrice Carter at the cemetery may not have any truth to it. Despite Marilyn's offer for Clara to come home with her that night to spend time with her and her family, Clara politely declined. She expressed the need to be alone for a while and to sleep in her and her late husband's bed that night. Clara mentioned she had a lot on her mind and would appreciate some time to process things before having a conversation with Marilyn. She thanked Marilyn for her offer and expressed her love for her daughter.

With that, Marilyn hugged her mom and told her how much she loved her and that she should call, day or night, if she needed help. Clara promised she would, and Marilyn left for home.

The following morning, there was heavy ice on the trees, the house, the barn, and the roads. The snow was still coming down, and the cold was still in Clara's heart. She moved around the house like a zombie, without purpose or meaning to her 44 years of existence with Sam. She received information about a 26-year-old event that she could neither confirm nor deny. The only one capable of explaining everything was now six feet under! The more she thought about it, the more she wanted to scream.

As Clara sat alone in the dimly lit living room, memories of her life with Sam flooded her mind. They had built a life together, raised children, and weathered countless storms. But now, a revelation from the past had shaken her to the core. The weight of uncertainty and unanswered questions burdened her soul.

Clara's thoughts drifted back to the day she received the mysterious information. It was a piece of the puzzle that didn't fit, a missing link in her life story. She felt lost and bewildered, grappling with emotions she couldn't quite understand. The truth seemed elusive, slipping through her fingers like melting snow.

With each passing moment, Clara's resolve grew stronger. She refused to let this revelation define her. She needed closure, answers to the questions that haunted her every waking moment. As the icy grip of winter held her home in its frigid embrace, Clara vowed to unravel the mystery that threatened to consume her.

Prophet of Doom

Harold Connors had spent the better part of his forty-eight years as a logger, beginning his journey alongside his father at the tender age of ten. He possessed an intimate knowledge of the logging trade and the art of making a living from it. Most of his days were now dedicated to marking timber across vast expanses of land, orchestrating the efforts of the sixteen men who labored tirelessly under the sun.

His company stood as the largest within a six-county realm, a source of immense pride for Harold, though it demanded exceedingly long hours and unwavering dedication. Together with his father, they had forged a reputation built on fairness, competitiveness, and productivity, earning the trust of the community with their timber. Yet, the work was fraught with peril, demanding vigilance and courage.

Sister Mabel, the devoted preacher at the Holiness Church of God in Round Oak, had held her position for eight remarkable years. Only twenty-eight, she was both skilled and devoted in her sermons, drawing the faithful to her altar calls, with many souls finding salvation week after week. Her presence exuded a certain allure that resonated deeply with her congregation. Living in the area with her husband, Zack, for most of their ten years of marriage, they had served various churches along their journey.

Every year, Mabel orchestrated a revival at her church, consistently yielding remarkable results. Her ability to save souls had garnered her fame, reaching even neighboring counties. Many local ministers envied her gift, as their services tended to be more rigid and structured. Mabel's gatherings were vibrant and alive, sometimes stretching for hours, with worshippers lost in song and spirit. She would preach passionately, interspersing hymns and performances by special singers, igniting a fervor that often led to jubilant expressions of faith, with some even speaking in tongues.

Zack would diligently collect offerings, counting the contributions after each collection to inform Sister Mabel whether they had met their weekly needs. It was not uncommon for Mabel to issue multiple altar calls, as there were always souls in need of redemption, even those who had found salvation the week prior.

In the back pew, my friends and I passed notes and shared sticks of Juicy Fruit chewing gum, the sweet treat beloved by the girls. This was our courtship ritual, a game to us boys, as we paid little heed to the sermons echoing around us. Our parents often turned to shush us, their gazes filled with disapproval as we disrupted the sanctity of the service.

Sister Mabel announced the annual Holy Ghost revival, set to unfold over the next two weeks. For me, it was an ordeal, as I, Allen Cross, lived just two blocks from the church with my mother, Mary. We attended every service until the doors closed, as Mama had experienced her own salvation within those walls. The small church, which accommodated seventy-five to eighty souls, often had chairs lined up in the aisles to welcome the influx of attendees during revivals.

For us youth, the revival was the highlight of the year, a social event where we delighted in witnessing who would respond to Mabel's altar calls. Snickers would ripple through our ranks whenever someone, perhaps a little less righteous, accepted Christ into their heart.

On a Monday morning, Harold rose early, burdened by a heavy quota he needed to meet by week's end. He often pondered how his father had managed such demands, recalling the late nights his father would return home, hastily eat, and disappear into sleep, only to rise before dawn to begin anew.

Six days a week, Harold worked tirelessly, reserving the Lord's Day for worship with his wife, Christy, a woman of unwavering faith. As a child, his parents dragged him to church every Sunday, making him sit with them on the front pew until he turned ten, when they finally allowed him to join the other kids in the back.

That was when I first became acquainted with Harold—a good kid, albeit misguided. We all thought well of him until he dared to flirt with Anna Sue, the girl of my dreams! I confronted him after church, demanding he leave her be, and he obliged, ensuring we had no further issues.

However, as high school progressed, Harold faced challenges, including a suspension for instigating a fight. After that incident, he seemed different, and we kept our distance.

After graduation, while Harold remained in logging, I ventured off to college. Our paths diverged until I returned home to work at a local CPA firm. Harold's father passed away when he was twenty-nine, leaving him at the helm of the family business. I was aware of the financial troubles that plagued Harold, often having to navigate shady dealings to keep the books balanced. He struggled with money management, and we frequently shuffled his funds to maintain appearances.

By thirty, Harold had transformed into a troubled man, embroiled in a tumultuous divorce. His wife had uncovered his infidelity, discovering he had a son out of wedlock with Donna Sellers, a local woman of dubious reputation. The townsfolk seemed to know before I did.

On Mother's Day, I attended church with my mother, where Sister Mabel announced an upcoming revival. I hadn't been to the Holiness Church in years; I had been devoted to First Baptist Church. The experience was starkly different, and I seldom attended the Holiness Church except on special occasions. Now, I served as a deacon at First Baptist, taking my role seriously, grateful for the foundations I had built in my youth.

"Next week, we'll welcome Sister Nita Roberts as our evangelist," Sister Mabel proclaimed, urging the congregation to invite others. Now aging, she had been the pastor for over forty years. "Remember, God will work in our hearts and our city, so spread the word!"

That week, I visited Harold's office to deliver documents for his signature. As we spoke about his unfortunate situation, I extended an invitation to the revival.

"It's a pure nightmare, Allen!" he lamented. "Not a day goes by that I don't regret my ignorance."

"I'd love for you to come back to Holiness Church for the revival. It's only a week long now, and Sister Mabel would be thrilled to see you. She promises not to call you out, but she'd like to pray for you."

At forty-eight, the logging industry had taken its toll on Harold, and I worried for him. I had heard whispers about his involvement with Patsy Sikes, and I knew that could lead to more trouble. So, as Sister Mabel wished, I shared the revival news, leaving the outcome to divine will.

I attended the revival with my mother, and to my surprise, Harold appeared that Sunday evening, sitting mid-way back with his old friend, Ricky Sparks. As the service unfolded, we sang hymns, offered prayers, and listened to Sister Nita deliver a powerful sermon on the prodigal son—a tale of loss, redemption, and the journey back to grace. The energy in the room swelled as the first altar call ignited an emotional outpouring, drawing cries and fervor from the congregation.

As the evening progressed, more singing and offerings followed, with the McGraw sisters captivating us with their melodies. Sister Nita's words resonated through the church, met with enthusiastic amens from the congregation.

When the second altar call arrived, Sister Judy Carter spoke in tongues, and Sister Mabel interpreted, the air thick with anticipation.

"God is telling someone in this congregation tonight that their soul is in danger of hell's fire unless they repent and turn to Jesus now," Sister Mabel declared.

All eyes turned, searching the congregation for the one meant to hear this message. I knew, and my gaze fell upon Harold. Though we should not judge, the weight of his recent choices pressed upon me, and I sensed the spirit beckoning him, much like the prodigal son.

After the service, I spoke with Harold, who seemed troubled and disturbed by the whole evening, believing salvation to be a deeply personal endeavor—not something anyone could impose on him.

The following day, news broke in our office of a tragic logging accident on Clark's Mill Road. A chill coursed through me, recalling Harold's struggle the night before. We awaited the confirmation of the victim's identity.

By noon, we learned it was Harold Connors. I rushed home to share the news with Anna Sue, my beloved wife, with whom I had finally united after years of longing. We prayed for Harold's soul, lamenting how I had hoped the prodigal would find his way to the altar the night prior. The choices we make define our paths, some leading us astray. I prayed Harold had followed Christ when he returned home that night.

You may call it coincidence, but I recognized the spirit's whisper through Sister Nita. She knew none of us, yet her words resonated deeply.

Doubt the existence of tongues? I do not anymore! The events of that revival lingered in my mind, a poignant reminder of the fragile nature of life and the profound impact of faith. Sister Nita's words, echoing through the church that night, felt like a divine intervention meant to steer Harold back onto a righteous path. As the days passed, I found myself reflecting on the importance of community and spiritual guidance in times of turmoil.

The logging community, tight-knit and resilient, rallied around Christy and Harold's children, offering support and comfort amidst their grief. It was a testament to the bonds formed through shared hardships and the solace found in collective strength. In the weeks following Harold's passing, Sister Mabel organized a special service in his memory, where friends and family gathered to celebrate his life and the legacy he left behind.

At the service, stories of Harold's kindness and generosity resurfaced, painting a portrait of a man who, despite his struggles, had touched many lives. It was a bittersweet occasion, filled with laughter and tears, as we all shared our favorite memories of him. I spoke of our childhood antics and the lessons learned along the way, grateful for the moments we had shared.

As I sat in the pew, hand in hand with Anna Sue, I realized that Harold's story was a powerful reminder of redemption and forgiveness. Though his journey had been fraught with challenges, it was not without hope. In the quiet moments of reflection, I prayed that his soul had found peace and that his legacy would inspire others to seek the light, even in the darkest of times.

Life in Round Oak continued, as it always did, with the rhythm of the seasons and the constant hum of daily life. The revival had stirred something within our community, a renewed commitment to faith and fellowship. Sister Mabel, ever the guiding light, continued her ministry with unwavering dedication, ensuring that the spirit of revival lived on in our hearts.

And so we carried on, holding onto the memories of those who had gone before us, drawing strength from their stories and the enduring power of faith.

Quietly in the Night

As the clock struck three-fifteen that fateful morning, Joe was roused from slumber by the insistent ring of his phone resting by his bedside. He reached out with urgency, recognizing the voice of his cherished friend, Bobby.

"Joe, there's a call from Fletcher's nursing home. They have a body."

With that, Joe slipped from the warmth of his bed, mindful not to disturb his wife, Doris, who had succumbed to a debilitating migraine the night before.

This marked Joe's twenty-first year of receiving such solemn summons, a duty that often called him at all hours. His heart resonated with reverence for his work at Mitchum's funeral home, a vocation he cherished as sacred and significant. Families in and around Sparksburg had entrusted him with their grief for many years. Each call initiated the profound process of care and counsel, a responsibility he held dear. He recalled his days in embalming school, where the first lesson was that the essence of their work lay in customer care. Each body they received was a cherished soul, deserving of the utmost dignity and respect.

Just the afternoon prior, Joe had visited his mother at Fletcher's. After suffering a massive stroke a month ago, she had shown signs of improvement, though her journey to recovery remained long. They had shared plans, including discussions about what would happen should her time come—a topic Joe had wished to avoid but assured her she would outlive him, a statement that brought a gentle smile to her face. A beloved figure, she had raised Joe alone from the age of five, following his father's passing from leukemia, which had left the family in a stable position because of his careful planning.

When the time came, his mother reassured him of her spiritual preparedness and readiness for death. They had exchanged affectionate kisses, and she had whispered her love before he departed.

As he dressed and made his way to the hearse parked behind the funeral home, Joe collected his keys to unlock the vehicle. The familiar routine continued as he picked up Bobby, just as they had done countless times before.

Bobby remarked, "I do not know who we're picking up. Marilyn didn't say when she called. We'll find out upon arrival."

Marilyn, the night nurse at the nursing home, had been a steadfast presence at Fletcher's for over forty years, sharing a long-standing friendship with Bobby, and their wives as well.

"Just remember, Bobby, whoever it is, let's not forget the paperwork this time. We need to get it right, unlike last week when we missed the forms."

"Yeah, I know, Joe. That was on me, and I own it. You know how it is; sometimes my mind races ahead of my actions," Bobby replied.

Turning onto Main Street and then right on Front, Joe navigated the familiar route to Fletcher's, the only nursing home in town, aged yet resilient, though in need of repairs.

They arrived at the back, where a ramp awaited their arrival, designed for such solemn pickups. Joe and Bobby had maneuvered many souls down that ramp, familiar with the bittersweet task. Bobby opened the hearse, extending the gurney, and together they approached the nurses' station just inside the rear entrance.

Marilyn greeted them with open arms, enveloping them in a heartfelt embrace. As she held Joe, tears glistened in her eyes. "Joe, I'm so sorry. It's your mom. She passed quietly in the night, free from pain. She chose her moment."

A wave of shock washed over Joe. Bobby placed a comforting hand on his shoulder, guiding him to a chair to gather his thoughts during this whirlwind of grief.

"I'm alright," Joe insisted. "This moment was always on the horizon. I'm taken aback to learn it's Mom. I'll manage; I have a duty to fulfill, and since it's *my* mother, I'd prefer to prepare her for her last voyage."

Both Marilyn and Bobby stood in silent support, unsure of how to navigate the weight of the moment. Eventually, Marilyn said to Joe, "I'm honored to help you with your mother. We've already prepared her body."

"Thank you, Marilyn," Joe replied. "Bobby, I'll need your assistance in placing her in the bag and rolling her out to the hearse," he said, feeling the pallor creep into his face.

"Whatever you need, Joe. I'm deeply sorry for your loss. Many cherished your mom," Bobby said earnestly.

Clarice Mallard, Joe's mother, had dedicated forty-two years to teaching fifth grade at Sparksburg Elementary, nurturing generations of students. In a town with limited employment opportunities, she had become a beloved figure, celebrated as "Teacher of the Year" multiple times.

Joe had faced the heart-wrenching decision to place his mother in Fletcher's following her stroke, knowing he couldn't balance home care with his job. It had been a struggle, but she was worth every sacrifice. The drive from Fletcher's to Mitchum's was heavy with sorrow.

Bobby, sensing the weight of the moment yet feeling compelled to ask, inquired, "Joe, do you want me to handle the embalming? It's usually better for us not to embalm our own, but I'll do whatever you want."

Joe pondered for a moment. "Bobby, as much as I appreciate your offer, I believe it's best to call on Horace Wilkes in Landsburg for the embalming. It just doesn't feel right for us to do it but thank you for understanding."

As they arrived at the funeral home, Deloris Jones, the long-time secretary, greeted them warmly, her compassion clear. She embraced Joe tightly, expressing her sorrow for Mrs. Clarice's passing.

"I truly appreciate that, Deloris," Joe said. "We have a lot of work ahead. Mom made her arrangements long ago, and it's our duty to honor them. I know you'll get started on contacting those who need to know, but we'll have to wait for Horace's arrival to determine the funeral arrangements."

Deloris nodded, understanding the gravity of the task ahead, and disappeared to gather the files.

After Joe and Bobby rolled Clarice into the embalming room and placed her in the cooler, Joe rushed to the office to call Doris, feeling a twinge of guilt for not contacting her sooner.

"Honey," he began as she answered, "I'm so sorry to tell you…"

But the words faltered as tears cascaded down his cheeks.

"Oh, sweetheart," Doris replied softly, "I'm so sorry about your mom. I'll get dressed and be there shortly. Just hold your head high, as your mom would want, and I'll be there as fast as I can."

"Okay, dear. Thank you," Joe replied, his voice breaking.

The funeral for Mrs. Clarice Mallard took place on a cold, dreary Tuesday afternoon in the quaint Methodist church where Joe and his mother had worshipped all their lives. The preacher, small and stooped, spoke glowingly of her as a wonderful mother, teacher, and devoted citizen.

An overflow crowd gathered to pay their respects, and after heartfelt tributes, they laid Clarice to rest in the family plot just outside Sparksburg at precisely three-fifteen in the afternoon. Joe stood by Doris, watching as the gravediggers returned to complete their solemn duty. This time, he was the one witnessing the finality of it all, a deeply personal moment.

Afterward, Joe approached Frank Sears and Leroy Salter, the gravediggers, offering them an extra fifty dollars each in gratitude for their often-overlooked contributions. They accepted with appreciation and drove off.

Joe lingered, gazing intently at the freshly turned earth, contemplating how swiftly life can shift—a mere heartbeat, and everything changes. He had navigated the waters of death throughout his life, yet this farewell felt uniquely challenging, marked by its undeniable finality.

As the night enveloped the world, the dedicated healthcare workers and funeral home staff continued their muted vigil, caring for those who had departed, often slipping away in the night's still. One day, we too shall embark on that journey. Prepare well, dear hearts. As Joe and Doris made their way back to their car, hand in hand, the gentle patter of rain fell, as if the heavens themselves were mourning alongside him. They drove home in silence, the weight of the day settling heavily on their shoulders.

Once home, Joe found solace in the familiar comfort of their living room, surrounded by the warmth of shared memories. Doris, ever the nurturing presence, brewed a pot of chamomile tea, knowing it was Joe's favorite remedy for a heavy heart. They sat together on the couch, the silence between them speaking volumes of shared understanding and love.

"Your mom was proud of you, Joe," Doris finally said, her voice soft and reassuring. "She raised a wonderful son who honors her legacy every day."

Joe nodded, a small smile forming despite the sorrow. "I just hope I can live up to everything she wanted for me."

"You already have," Doris replied, squeezing his hand gently.

As the evening wore on, Joe reflected on the moments he had shared with his mother, her laughter, her wisdom, and the unwavering support she had given him throughout his life. He resolved to carry her spirit forward, to continue the work he loved, and to find peace in knowing she was now at rest.

In the days that followed, the community of Sparksburg rallied around Joe and Doris, offering their condolences, and sharing fond memories of Clarice. The outpouring of love and support was a testament to the impact she had made during her lifetime.

With each passing day, the sting of loss softened, replaced by a sense of gratitude for having had such a remarkable woman as his mother. Joe knew that while she was gone, her legacy lived on in the hearts of all who had known her.

As the weeks turned into months, Joe returned to his duties at Mitchum's funeral home with renewed purpose, honoring each departed soul with the same care and compassion his mother had instilled in him. In the quiet moments, he would often look up and whisper a silent thank you to the woman who had shaped his life in so many profound ways.

And so, life in Sparksburg continued, marked by the rhythms of joy and sorrow, beginnings, and endings, all woven together in the tapestry of human experience.

"Repaint, Ye Thinners!"

"Repent ye: for the kingdom of heaven is at hand."
(Matthew 3:2 KJV)

Clyde and Terry, both skilled artisans of the brush, had been laboring tirelessly at Saint Peter's Episcopal Church for a week, their hearts set on the completion of their masterpiece as the sun dipped low on a Friday afternoon. Eager for their reward, they climbed their towering thirty-foot extension ladder to paint the last section of the roof, the heat of July causing steam to rise from the asphalt shingles beneath them.

After a long week of toil, they delayed painting the steeple until they finished painting every other surface. It loomed before them, a formidable challenge standing fifteen feet tall, crafted entirely of wood, crowned by a delicate cross that reached for the heavens.

Their paint supply dwindled, and uncertainty clouded their minds—would the remnants of a couple of gallons suffice for the steeple's grandeur? The paint shop lay twenty-two miles away in Dover, its doors destined to close before they could fetch more, leaving them to confront the encroaching darkness without fresh supplies. Urgency clawed at them; they *had* to receive payment *today*, for their bills lay overdue, and the relentless hounds of obligation were already at their door!

Then Clyde conjured what he deemed a brilliant solution. "Terry, why not mix some water into our paint and see if that'll stretch it for the steeple? Nobody down there will notice!"

"Tis the finest idea you've had all week," Terry replied, a hint of skepticism lacing his words. "But let's ponder this: we're in a church, and might we anger God by skimping on the paint? Does that not trouble you?"

"Naw!" Clyde retorted confidently. "God ain't in the painting business, so why should it vex Him how we adorn this steeple?"

"Just saying," Terry replied. "We've been away from church so long; God might've forgotten us, but I'll roll with your plan this time. I can't wait to finish and head to Billy Bob's for a cold beer!"

"I'm with you for sure," Clyde exclaimed. "The first round's on me!"

With their pact sealed, Clyde secured the ladder against the steeple and tied it with rope, while Terry combined the remaining paint, mixing in water before handing the concoction to Clyde. They had affixed a toe board to the roof for stability, giving Clyde a sense of security.

"Be careful, Clyde, and tie yourself to the steeple when you reach the top. I won't be able to catch you if you fall!" Terry cautioned.

"Not a problem," Clyde replied, ever optimistic.

With paint can and brush in hand, Clyde ascended toward the pinnacle of the steeple, needing to stretch beyond the last rung of the ladder to paint the cross above. It was a precarious endeavor, but Clyde had faced such feats before.

As he completed the cross on all sides, his legs trembled with the effort, yet he methodically whitewashed the spire, inching his way down, repositioning the toe board and ladder with each side.

When he reached the last side, the rumble of distant thunder echoed ominously. A storm approached, yet Clyde's determination held firm. Dark clouds gathered above the quaint church as he stood atop the last section, lightning flashing perilously close, raising his concern for safety.

And then it happened. Gazing up at the menacing cloud, Clyde witnessed a last bolt of lightning illuminate the darkness, revealing a message scrawled across the sky.

"Do you see those words up there, Terry?" Clyde called out; eyes wide with wonder.

"I ain't seen nothing," Terry replied, puzzled. "What in tarnation are you talking about, Clyde?"

"I see it!" Clyde exclaimed. "It's right there in the cloud!"

"Well, what does it say, wise guy?" Terry pressed.

Clyde squinted again, straining to decipher the celestial message, and proclaimed aloud the *emblazoned* words: ***REPAINT, YE THINNERS!***

The message hung there, a celestial command that seemed to echo through the very fibers of Clyde's being. He blinked, half expecting the vision to vanish like a mirage, yet the words remained stark against the swirling gray.

Terry, still skeptical, chuckled. "You sure you ain't dehydrated, Clyde? Maybe that steeple's closer to heaven than we thought."

Clyde, however, felt a chill that had nothing to do with the approaching storm. "No, Terry, this is a sign. We shouldn't have diluted that paint. What if we're being told to do it right?"

Terry paused, the weight of Clyde's words settling over him like the gathering storm clouds. "Are you saying we should head to Dover and get the proper supplies, even if it means delaying our payment?"

Clyde nodded, his resolve firm. "Better to paint it right and face the music than ignore a message from above."

With a shared nod of understanding, the two men descended the ladder, their decision made. As they packed up their tools and prepared to leave, the rain fell, gently at first, then with increasing fervor, washing away the remnants of their thinned paint.

They drove to Dover in silence, each man lost in his thoughts. Yet beneath the silence lay a sense of peace, as if by choosing integrity, they had aligned themselves with a greater purpose. They might face a hard conversation with the church board, but they would do so knowing that they had heeded the call to do what was right.

As they pulled into the paint shop just before closing, the sky cleared, and a rainbow arched across the horizon, a gentle reminder that sometimes, the path to redemption begins with a single stroke of a brush.

Final Harvest

In the verdant tapestry of agriculture, Roger stood as a virtuoso, crafting harmony amid the challenges of modern corporate farming. Each year, he cultivated a dazzling array of crops—Vidalia sweet onions, seedless watermelons, hybrid corn, soybeans, peanuts, wheat, and Bermuda hay for his cherished cattle. Mastering the art of no-till farming, he became the envy of local cultivators. As spring blossomed, he surveyed his expansive fields like a maestro gazing upon his orchestra, ready to orchestrate nature's bounty. The exhilaration of breaking the loamy soil, inhaling its rich fragrance, and envisioning the harvest to come filled his heart with joy. With each movement of his hands, he conjured magic across countless acres.

In perfect synchrony, he drove his trusted John Deere tractor, crafting a symphony in the fields. Though tempted by the allure of a new machine, he felt that old Betsy still had a few good seasons left in her.

For generations, Roger's family had nurtured these vast lands, and each year he expanded his reach, leasing more fields to amplify his yield. His workforce swelled to over a hundred, and his state-of-the-art processing plant buzzed with activity. Trucks journeyed from Pennsylvania, New England, Arkansas, Colorado, and beyond to buy his prized red-meat watermelons and delectable Vidalia sweet onions. His enterprise flourished, and his renown as a farmer spread everywhere. Each year, the State of Georgia's Department of Agriculture visited to glean insights from Roger's innovative techniques, sharing his wisdom with fellow farmers across the state.

Maribel, Roger's beloved wife of forty-two years, was his steadfast partner, accountant, and confidante. Though they had tried in vain to welcome children into their lives, their bond remained unbreakable. Together, they worked tirelessly from dawn till dusk, driven by a shared purpose and love for the land.

But then, fate took a cruel turn. In this otherwise idyllic existence, a persistent pain in Roger's neck intensified. Initially dismissing it as a mere strain from his labor, he resorted to an old remedy his father had once used—a pungent balm that offered fleeting relief. Maribel, concerned for her husband's well-being, urged him to consult their family physician, but Roger, steadfast in his belief that the fields required his attention, resisted her pleas. She often chided him for his frugality, yet he continued to shoulder the burden of his work, ignoring the growing discomfort.

Any farmer would attest to the daunting financial risks tied to their craft—the cost of fertilizer, fuel, seeds, and labor loom heavy, with the potential for loss always lurking. Brian Brett aptly remarked, "Farming is a profession of hope." Each season, farmers stake their livelihoods on the promise of a bountiful harvest, praying for favorable weather and market conditions.

Many lament the price of food at the market, but farmers would advise against complaining with mouths full. The toil that goes into each crop is immeasurable.

The ancient philosopher Xenophon declared, "Agriculture, for an honorable and high-minded man, is the best of all occupations or arts by which men buy the means of living." As the child of a sharecropper, I hold profound respect for farmers, having witnessed my father's labor in the fields—harvesting corn, cucumbers, watermelons, peas, butter beans, and okra. I remember our sleepless nights at the state farmer's market, taking turns selling our produce, often dozing atop the watermelons.

I walked alongside my father as he guided our steadfast mule, Bessie, who expertly laid straight rows for planting. Our family's survival depended on those market trips and the success of our crops.

A tale is told of a young boy who approached an old farmer on his porch, whittling a stick. The boy asked, "How are your crops doing this year?" The old farmer replied, "Didn't plant anything this year. I decided to just play it safe!" Many farmers resonate with that sentiment, for the daunting task of investing in a crop without knowing the whims of nature can be paralyzing. Rain is vital, yet too much can spell disaster. Each night, farmers pray for favorable skies, hoping for a bountiful dawn.

Debbie Stabenow noted, "Agriculture looks different today. Our farmers are using GPS [Global Positioning System], and you can monitor your irrigation systems from anywhere over the internet." Roger embraced these advancements, growing into the largest farming operation in the county, a pillar of support for many. Yet, he often lay awake at night, consumed by worries about his future.

Then, without warning, Roger awoke, gripped by a searing pain that radiated through his neck and into his head. His left eye twitched uncontrollably, prompting Maribel to assist him. Recognizing the urgency, she quickly dressed and drove him thirty miles to the nearest hospital, where doctors swiftly placed him under stroke protocol and subjected him to a series of tests, including a brain scan.

But the storm had already broken; Roger suffered a massive stroke, and despite resuscitation efforts, he slipped away from this world. The physician's assistant delivered the devastating news to Maribel, who collapsed beside her chair in the waiting area, her heart shattered.

No more fields to tend. No more worries about weather or market fluctuations. No more machinery to repair or workers to manage. Roger had completed his final harvest, leaving behind a legacy woven into the very fabric of the land he loved.

The vast fields, holding memories of their shared dreams and endeavors, surrounded Maribel as she navigated the aftermath. The community, which had long admired Roger's dedication and ingenuity, rallied around her, offering support and solace in her time of grief.

As she walked through the fields, Maribel felt Roger's presence in every rustle of the wind and every sunbeam that kissed the earth. She vowed to honor his memory by continuing the work they had started together. With the help of their loyal workers and the guidance of Roger's meticulous records, she took on the challenge of managing the farm.

In the months that followed, Maribel discovered a strength she never knew she possessed. She became a beacon of resilience and determination, not just for her family, but for the entire farming community. Under her stewardship, the farm continued to thrive, a testament to the enduring spirit of the man she loved and the legacy they built together.

Though the pain of losing Roger remained, Maribel found comfort in the rhythm of the seasons and the knowledge that he was still with her, tending the fields and watching over the land they cherished.

Familiar Things

Corey Carter was a creature of delightful habit, weaving the threads of his life in a tapestry of routine. Living at 2417 Lisbon Street in the quaint embrace of the old town, he shared his days with his beloved wife of seventeen years, Maryanne. A diligent bank insurance salesperson, Maryanne had dedicated fifteen years to her profession, ensuring the cloak of insurance shielded those venturing into homeownership or purchasing vehicles. Yet, beneath her composed exterior lay the weight of obsessive-compulsive tendencies that had accompanied her for years. Early in their union, they had chosen the path of childlessness, believing that little ones might cast shadows upon their uncomplicated lives. Their days unfolded in a harmonious rhythm, where the alarm clock signaled not only the start and end of their daily rituals, but also the essence of their mutual contentment.

Their charming cottage, a modest two-bedroom dwelling constructed in 1967, stood at the end of Lisbon Street, a serene sanctuary amidst the surrounding grandeur. Across the way loomed a stately four-bedroom mansion at 2415 Lisbon, languishing unsold for three years, while next door at 2419, the Stryker brothers—Carl and William—called a three-bedroom ranch home. Though the couple found solace in their quaint abode, the imposing homes on either side sometimes threatened to overshadow their happiness. Yet, they thrived in their simplicity, reveling in the joy of their shared existence.

Maryanne had stumbled upon their cottage through the bank, where her supervisor had offered them the opportunity to acquire it at a remarkably low interest rate of $65,000, a veritable steal for the Lisbon neighborhood. They cherished this fortuitous bargain, crafting a home filled with love and care.

Their yard blossomed into a vibrant showcase, a testament to their shared dedication. Corey had planted two red maples flanking the entrance, and behind them bloomed a kaleidoscope of pansies in winter and a plethora of daylilies, Mexican petunias, dusty millers, and crocus in springtime. Corey tended to each blade of grass with reverence. Diligent in his stewardship, Corey kept his verdant domain a lush oasis year-round. Their efforts bore fruit, earning them the coveted "Yard of the Month" title on two occasions, a badge of pride displayed in their garden.

Corey's mornings began with the gentle embrace of dawn. Rising around five, he would tiptoe from their shared sanctuary, careful not to disturb Maryanne's slumber. In the kitchen, he would prepare his cherished cup of Gevalia Colombian coffee, bold and dark, served black, much to Maryanne's occasional chagrin when he pilfered the first cup before the pot was complete. His beloved, hand-painted rooster mug, though cracked and weary, held a special place in his heart, for he believed coffee tasted best within its embrace.

Maryanne, a woman of few complaints, devoted herself to her work. Recently offered the role of assistant bank manager, she debated the opportunity with Corey, who encouraged her without hesitation. She feared that longer hours and less time together would cost them their cherished simplicity.

Corey, secure in his position at Lockheed, relished the camaraderie of his coworkers and the stability of his role. He had thrived there for fifteen years, ascending to the position of line supervisor, where his colleagues found comfort in his presence. Each evening, he returned home to change into work clothes and ride his John Deere mower, a ritual he cherished as much as life itself. He believed it was a man's duty to maintain the lawn, and he kept Maryanne at bay from this chore.

Together, Corey and Maryanne enjoyed the rhythm of life, exercising three times weekly and walking two miles while sharing their thoughts. Sundays were sacred, reserved for worship at First Presbyterian Church, where they found solace in Pastor Johnson's gentle words, avoiding the complexities of politics and deeper discussions.

Yet, as time flowed, questions lingered in the shadows of their hearts. Was their bond genuinely love? They had known each other since high school, and their relationship blossomed into a union marked by safety and comfort. But love, with its myriad definitions, often eluded them. Their connection mirrored the lyrics of Tina Turner's "What's

Love Got to Do with It?"—rooted in mutual care more than fiery passion.

As the years unfolded, the winds of change whispered. Maryanne, plagued by a persistent ache in her left rib cage, initially dismissed it as trivial. But when excruciating pain struck one fateful evening, Corey rushed her to Macon General. There, amidst the sterile walls, a doctor discovered an abnormality.

The following Monday, as they awaited Dr. Brown's verdict, anxiety danced between them. Corey, ever the optimist, offered reassurances that did little to quell Maryanne's frantic thoughts. They entered the examination room, where Dr. Brown greeted them with a calm demeanor, yet the gravity of the situation weighed heavily.

"Your stress test results are concerning," he said, a hint of worry in his voice. "I recommend immediate hospitalization for a catheterization to understand the underlying issues."

Maryanne's heart raced, conjuring images of the Titanic's last moments, fearing for Corey's future without her. Yet, amid her turmoil, Corey remained a steadfast beacon of support, promising they would navigate the storm together.

As Maryanne prepared for her procedure, Corey found solace in the chapel's quiet embrace, praying fervently for her safety. A warm, reassuring hand clasped his in a moment that felt transcendent—an encounter that left him pondering whether it was divine intervention.

After the surgery, Dr. Sizemore emerged with news of a large anterior mediastinal mass found beneath Maryanne's breastbone. "It may be benign," he assured them, "but we need to proceed with caution."

In the days that followed, as they navigated a whirlwind of emotions, Maryanne expressed her fears of losing everything—her job, her life, and her beloved Corey. Yet, he remained her anchor, promising that they would face whatever came their way together.

When the day of surgery arrived, Maryanne's heartfelt words, "Whatever happens, Corey, always remember that I love you," resonated deeply within him. He held her hand through the double doors, a promise forged in love and unwavering hope.

As the hours stretched on, Corey waited, his heart filled with prayers and anticipation. When at last Maryanne awoke, he reassured her, recounting the extraordinary warmth he had felt in the chapel, a sign of God's presence in their darkest hour.

With each passing day, Maryanne's strength returned, and they embraced the life they had built together. Though they returned to their routines, the warmth of that hand lingered in Corey's heart, a reminder of faith's power and love's enduring light, guiding them through the trials that lay ahead.

In the months that followed, Corey and Maryanne discovered a renewed appreciation for the simple joys that had always defined their lives. Their morning coffees, once a mere routine, now felt like cherished rituals, a time to savor each other's company and reflect on the blessings they had. The walks they took, hand in hand, became more than just exercise; they were moments of profound connection, where words were often unnecessary, and the shared silence spoke volumes.

The garden, too, became a symbol of resilience and rebirth. With Maryanne's recovery, she found solace in tending to the flowers, each bloom a testament to the beauty that emerges even after the harshest storms. Corey, ever the diligent gardener, found joy in watching her rediscover the passions that fear and uncertainty had once overshadowed.

At the bank, Maryanne's colleagues greeted her with open arms and heartfelt support, having rallied around her during her absence. She embraced the role of assistant manager, finding a newfound confidence in balancing the demands of work with the precious time she now cherished more than ever with Corey.

As for Corey, his perspective on life had shifted. He returned to Lockheed with a greater appreciation for his colleagues and the stability his job provided. The camaraderie he experienced there was stronger, and he found himself more engaged, more present, grateful for the support they had shown him during Maryanne's ordeal.

Sundays at First Presbyterian became even more meaningful. Pastor Johnson's words resonated deeply, and the couple found solace in the community that had become like family. They took part in church activities with renewed enthusiasm, eager to give back to those who had given them so much support.

Through it all, the question of love's nature had found its answer in their trials. It was in the muted strength they offered one another, in the sacrifices made, and in the unwavering support that transcended spoken words. They learned that love, unlike grand gestures or fiery passion, lived in a partner's steadfast presence as they journeyed through life's uncertainties.

As spring blossomed once again in their garden, Corey and Maryanne knew that the winds of change would always blow, but they were ready to face whatever came next, hand in hand, with love as their guiding light.

RELIGION AND PHILOSOPHY

Whether religion is man-made is a question for philosophers or theologians. But the forms are man-made. They are a human response to something. As a historian of religions, I am interested in those expressions.

—Mircea Eliade, AZ Quotes

Under the Canopy

In my enchanting backyard, a tapestry of trees, bushes, plants, and flowers unfolds, featuring camellias, Thuja green giants, towering pines, and a myriad of other botanical wonders. It stands as a microcosm of nature, nurturing the myriad creatures that call it home.

To me, this sanctuary reflects the grand narrative of life itself. Amid the vibrant growth of trees and bushes, there lies the duality of existence—beauty intertwined with peril. Each day reveals both the blossoming of new life and the shadow of danger lurking at every corner.

On a crisp spring morning, I retreat to the cool shade of my majestic elm tree. The wind whispers gently at five miles per hour, while the sun ascends, casting its golden glow over the horizon. With a steaming cup of coffee cradled in my hands, I attune myself to the symphony of morning sounds. Beneath the protective canopy, squirrels scamper from branch to branch, diligently seeking their first meal. Their relentless pursuit mirrors our own ancestors, driven by the primal need for sustenance. The cycle of life unfolds ceaselessly, as we are born, strive, and eventually depart. For some, this rhythm is a dream; for others, it is a relentless torment.

A blue jay swoops down, delivering breakfast to its young nestled in one of my camellias. Their tiny voices, filled with pleading cries, remind me of their fragility and dependency on their parents. Soon, they will venture forth, embarking on their own journeys, seeking partners, building nests, and nurturing new families—an exquisite portrayal of the life cycle's progression.

A red-tailed hawk shattered the tranquility; it descended, snatched the unsuspecting dove in its talons, and soared into the nearby woods to feast and care for its own brood. The humble dove, so gentle, becomes a stark reminder of nature's harsh realities.

Such is life in all its wondrous and perplexing glory, where beauty and cruelty coexist. Witnessing the dance of existence—both life and death—can be challenging, yet it is the divine design of our world.

Human dangers lurk beneath this canopy as well. We have encountered copperhead moccasins and recently dealt with a rogue pit bull that claimed fifty of our neighbor's chickens. Amidst all this splendor, danger persists. I observe a tiny caterpillar inching its way up the trunk of my elm, while a pileated woodpecker flits from tree to tree, extracting insects from every crevice. Its striking red and white feathers flash as it makes its distinctive rat-a-tat sound, burrowing deeper into the decaying pine nearby.

As the sun rises higher, a flock of Canadian geese glides overhead, journeying from one pond to another, where they will feast along the water's edge. Mother Nature has provided them with all they need—a delicate balance of existence.

After several days without rain, the canopy appears parched, prompting me to activate my sprinkler system to quench its thirst. I see myself as the guardian of this verdant realm, embracing my responsibility with reverence.

As the sun brightens, I sip my coffee and notice the bustling activity around me. Overnight, little critters have fashioned mounds across the yard, teeming with life. Ants, both welcome and unwelcome, contribute to the ecosystem while reminding me of life's bittersweet nature. If only we could coexist without causing each other harm, yet the truth remains: every being has a role to fulfill, a journey to undertake.

Upon setting out my bird feeder, a delightful array of species gathers, and I am mesmerized by their grace as they flit to the feeder and soar into the azure sky. I take pride in providing for them.

One morning, while watering flowers with a sprinkler hose, a splendid ruby-throated hummingbird dances in the water's mist, expressing its delight. It flits to the hummingbird feeders on our porch, which we refill regularly. Their arrival each March is a joyful spectacle, though they can be quite territorial over the nectar.

Just recently, while adjusting their feeders, one daring hummingbird darted at me, as if to scold. I thought, "Oh little one, if only you knew I am your provider." Yet, such is the nature of life. Humans often overlook the contributions of those who nourish us. As the proverb goes, "We complain about farmers with our mouths full." Gratitude often eludes us amidst our blessings.

As the sun climbs higher, I retreat indoors to escape the heat, leaving the canopy and its delicate balance behind. Tasks await—places to go, people to meet. Life's rhythm continues until the day arrives, when news of a friend's passing jolts us into reflection. This compels us to reassess our lives and the time we have left. The existence beneath the canopy is fragile yet authentic, where we spend our days and find our essence.

Recently, a documentary, *Death Makes Life Possible*, captivated me; it showed how one thing gives life to another—like leaves falling in autumn, nourishing the soil that supports future growth. As I gaze at the canopy, I ponder the fallen leaves that will feed the myriad creatures relying on them for sustenance and shelter.

John Lithgow in *The Crown* poignantly remarked, "We are all dying. That defines the condition of living." Acknowledging this truth, we should embrace the gift of life while we still can. The universe, in all its marvelous complexity, could not have been born of mere chance.

I cherish the adage, "God must have a sense of humor when He created man." This uniqueness of life beneath the canopy—the myriad races, colors, and personalities—fills me with gratitude. I will live and die under this verdant expanse, savoring each new day and my steaming morning mug of coffee. Life indeed could not be sweeter.

As I sit here reflecting on the tapestry of life that unfolds in my backyard, I am reminded of the interconnectedness of all living things. Each creature, from the smallest ant to the soaring hawk, plays a vital role in the grand scheme of existence. This intricate web of life is a testament to the delicate balance that sustains us all, a balance that we must strive to protect and nurture.

In this serene sanctuary, I find solace and inspiration. The beauty of the natural world is a constant reminder of the wonders that surround us, urging us to appreciate the simple joys of life. As I watch the sunlight filter through the leaves, casting dancing shadows on the ground, I am filled with a sense of peace and contentment.

This backyard, with its vibrant flora and fauna, is more than just a piece of land; it is a living, breathing entity that offers lessons in resilience, adaptation, and harmony. Each day spent under its canopy is a gift, an opportunity to reconnect with the earth and reflect on our place within it.

As the day draws to a close, and the sun dips below the horizon, painting the sky in hues of pink and orange, I am grateful for the moments of tranquility and reflection this space offers. In the evening's quiet, as the stars twinkle above, I am reminded of the vastness of the universe and the preciousness of each fleeting moment.

In this ever-changing world, my backyard remains a constant, a reminder of the enduring beauty and complexity of life. It is here that I find my center, my grounding, and my inspiration to face each new day with hope and gratitude. Life indeed could not be sweeter.

THE MEANING OF OUR LIVES

In the first century B.C., the Roman poet Ovid wisely observed, "You can't catch a fish unless your fly is in the water." It is high time I cast my line. Seventy years have flowed into the creation of this book, and it is now time to give those years substance by imparting the knowledge and discoveries I have accumulated along the way. With a treasure trove of memories nestled somewhere in the recesses of my mind, I shall pen the momentous events that have shaped my journey. I hope that my children, grandchildren, and all who follow will find solace or inspiration in the words I weave.

During the COVID-19 pandemic, I ventured to Wrightsville, Georgia, to pay my respects at the grave of a dear friend. Dr. Richard T. Brantley, a former faculty member at the New Orleans Theological Seminary, was a beacon of wisdom who taught Hebrew and shepherded several Baptist congregations throughout his life. Together with three other friends, he and I established a rock gospel band during our college days.

As I stood by my friend's grave, I noticed the headstone bore a brief dash between his birth and death. In that moment, I realized I was part of that dash—a representation of the lives we lived and the connections we forged. Life is too fleeting for frivolity or waste. In the sweltering summer heat of South Georgia, I grasped at seventy, the ephemeral nature of existence and felt an urgent call to immerse myself in the waters of life. This inspired me to author this book.

Gwyneth Paltrow, in the film *View from the Top*, remarked, "Life is a series of arrivals and departures." I have arrived, while my friend Ricky has departed. It is time to abandon excuses and embrace life while the sun still shines. I am determined to cherish each moment, uplift those around me, love abundantly, and place trust in myself and others.

Before a championship Little League game, Keanu Reeves, in his role as a coach, told his team, "One of the most important things in life is just showing up." Each new day holds the promise of being the best day of my life. I shall strive to make a difference in all that I do by simply being present and using the gifts bestowed upon me by God. Though I may not master any field, I will strive to do my best and bless others as God has blessed me.

Burt Reynolds poignantly stated in *The Last Movie Star*, "Everybody knows how the movie ends, but it's the scenes in the middle that make it count." This brings us back to the dash, that minuscule mark signifying the chapters of our lives. Many live ensconced in fear or isolation, missing the vibrant scenes life offers. They allow worries and challenges to cloud their path, diverting them from becoming the dash they were.

Consider the odds that are impossible to beat: envision a small box turtle inching toward a four-lane highway with a wide median. The other day, I spotted one, and I marveled at its bravery—or folly—in attempting to cross such a perilous expanse. Yet, with tenacity and courage, it pressed on. Whatever the label, the choice lies with you.

In the film *Rudy*, a young man named Rudy, dreams of playing football for his beloved Notre Dame Fighting Irish. Hailing from a modest background, he faces numerous obstacles but continues to pursue his dream. After much perseverance, he finds himself on the practice squad, enduring challenges yet never losing sight of his goal.

During his senior year, amid chants of his name ringing through the stadium, Rudy is granted the opportunity to play in the last moments of the game. Despite his small stature, he made impactful tackles, leading his team to victory, and they celebrated him as a hero. The pride of his parents shines through, and it's impossible not to tear up at his triumph.

Reflect on Erik Weihenmayer, who in 2001 became the first blind person to conquer Mount Everest at thirty-three. His story, featured on the *Today* show and in *Time* magazine, captured the essence of "Blind Faith." His unwavering spirit propelled him to heights where many sighted individuals faltered. While we often settle for the ordinary, he dared to seek the extraordinary.

Then there's Alex Honnold, who famously scaled El Capitan in Yosemite without safety ropes. His audacity and skill astonished me as I witnessed his feats through a powerful telescope. Although I've hiked parts of the Appalachian Trail, Honnold's achievements are still much more impressive.

"Nothing ventured, nothing gained," as the adage goes. This truth resonates with the endeavors of NASA, which achieved the monumental feat of landing on the moon. Without the faith and confidence of those involved, such a triumph would have remained a dream.

In high school, I vividly recall an elderly World War II veteran, known as "Cart Man," who lived in a modest house without electricity or running water. Despite the hardships he faced after losing both legs in the war, he pushed himself into town daily to enjoy coffee with friends and share his faith. His determination inspired awe as he traversed the distance with grit and resolve.

One day, as I walked home, he spoke with me. Despite his worn attire and wobbly cart, he shared the wisdom that has lingered in my heart. "Throughout life, we all bear our burdens, but some let those burdens weigh them down." When I asked why he made the daily journey, he replied, "Should I just stay at home and die? I have one chance at this life, and I intend to make the most of it."

I expressed how impressed my classmates were by his spirit, and he thanked me. As he slowly continued his journey, I could hear him softly repeating, "It was good talking to you."

There are countless souls like Cart Man, navigating life in search of connection.

Focusing on your inner self: What compels you? What compels you to rise each day and confront life's challenges? What aspirations do you hold? Do you possess the same resilience as Cart Man to believe you can make a difference?

"Life is not primarily a quest for pleasure," Sigmund Freud once said, nor merely a pursuit of power, as Alfred Adler taught, but a quest for meaning. Victor Frankl, a Holocaust survivor, understood this deeply. He faced unimaginable horrors, yet emerged with a profound understanding of life's purpose.

Frankl posited three sources of meaning: in work, love, and courage during trials. "The way we respond to suffering gives our pain meaning," he wrote. While we may not control our circumstances, we can choose our responses.

"Two men looked through prison bars; one saw mud, the other saw stars." This phrase has guided me through life, reminding me I can influence the world around me. Though I may feel small, my existence can spark change for others. We must not traverse life selfishly; instead, we should strive to be catalysts for transformation.

The Cart Man embodies the spirit of Victor Frankl. It is through our actions, the love we share, and the risks we embrace, that we uncover the true meaning of our lives.

As I continue this reflection, I am reminded of the countless individuals who have touched my life and left indelible marks on my soul. I weave their stories, much like the Cart Man's, into the tapestry of my existence, adding richness and depth to my journey.

Each encounter, whether fleeting or enduring, has offered lessons that have shaped who I am today. From the laughter shared with childhood friends to the wisdom imparted by mentors, every moment has been a brushstroke on the canvas of my life.

I recall the vibrant sunsets observed from my porch, moments of solitude that have offered clarity and peace. Nature, in its infinite beauty, has always been a source of inspiration, reminding me of the vastness of the world and the interconnectedness of all living things.

As I pen these words, I strive to honor those who have walked beside me, whether for a brief chapter or the entirety of my story. Their courage, kindness, and resilience have been a guiding light, illuminating the path ahead.

May these reflections serve not only as a testament to a life well-lived, but also as a beacon for those seeking direction amidst life's uncertainties. Let us all endeavor to live with purpose, embracing the unknown with open hearts and minds, ever ready to cast our lines into the waters of possibility.

THINGS TO LIVE BY

I consider myself a philosopher of sorts, ever ready to engage in spirited debates on any topic! I cherish profound conversations about life and navigate the labyrinth of complex mental challenges.

We often misinterpret life, a complex tapestry, as a simple undertaking. Many ancient sages believed only a handful of truths should guide our existence. Here, I seek to illuminate the four essential elements I have gleaned through years of philosophical exploration.

#1. It is essential to have a place to be.

We all sail the vast sea of life, navigating uncharted waters. Daily, we seek that haven where we belong. I've learned that chasing unrealistic aspirations can lead to turmoil. My life with my beloved wife, Renee, is a testament to commitment; we vowed long ago, before a minister, to journey together through life. In contrast, many today embark on relationships that seem destined for discord. Statistics reveal a staggering 50 percent of marriages end in divorce. What lies at the heart of this dilemma? It's that modern souls have become more self-absorbed than those of yore, losing sight of the importance of mutual inclusion in life's plans.

As we strive for our desired destinations, life often intervenes with its myriad disruptions. We encounter many circumstances and complexities in life. Embracing change is vital when intertwining our lives with another. Renee and I engage in daily compromises, deciding together that shape our journey. When unified in our efforts, the turbulent waters of life become far more navigable.

Thus, we yearn for that ideal sanctuary. I have discovered mine, rich not in gold but in the love of two grown children and two grandchildren. Our lives now revolve around them, a choice made years ago when we embraced parenthood. This decision required us to relinquish many personal ambitions, yet it brought immeasurable joy.

Although I never envisioned myself as a minister, divine providence had other plans. God called me to share the gospel, allowing me to pursue my passion for country music through church singing, songwriting, and recording. For fifty-two years, I have embraced this path, thriving in the love of life, God, and those around me—leading me to the second vital truth.

#2. It is vital to have someone to love.

The esteemed John Donne captured this truth eloquently: "No man is an island..." We thrive best when enveloped in the warmth of love from those who care for us. We are not solitary beings; love is a shared journey.

Renowned philosopher Roman Krznaric explored six types of love in his work, *How Should We Live?*

- **Eros**: the flame of passion and desire

- **Philia**: the bonds of friendship and family

- **Ludus**: the playful affection among children

- **Pragma**: a mature love that strengthens over time

- **Agape**: selfless love, a giving spirit

- **Philautia**: self-love or narcissism

We each resonate with these forms of love. My bond with Renee embodies agape love, while my devotion to Christ and the church reflects this selfless spirit. Philia love enriches most of us through our friends and family, while those ensnared in philautia focus on themselves. My grandparents, united by circumstance in the 1920s, eventually cultivated a deep pragma love over the years.

Eros love, often dramatized in media, emphasizes passion and desire, while ludus love shines through the innocent joy of children. Throughout our lives, we may experience a symphony of these loves, intertwining and enriching our existence. We all need someone to love.

#3. It is crucial to have someone who loves you.

To fill the voids in our hearts, those who genuinely care for our well-being must surround us. Renee stands by me, but I ponder the emptiness I would feel if she were ever absent. Fortunately, I am blessed with family, church members, and countless friends who also love me. Living without such connections would be a profound sadness. While some claim they prefer solitude, often it stems from past wounds, leading them to forgo the chance at renewed relationships—a truly tragic existence.

#4. Finally, it is vital to have someone or something to believe in.

My wife believes in my potential to bring this book to life, serving as my proofreader, advisor, and steadfast companion. She has supported me in my ministry for over fifty years, nurturing my growth. I am eternally grateful for her unwavering presence.

Thus, I present to you a place to be, someone to love, someone who loves you, and someone or something to believe in. While other ideas may resonate with you, these four truths stand as pillars of a fulfilling life. May you be well, and may blessings abound.

In reflecting on these four guiding principles, I appreciate they are not just abstract concepts, but tangible experiences that shape our daily lives. They serve as anchors in the unpredictable ocean of existence, providing stability and direction.

Having a place to be grounds us, providing a sense of belonging and purpose. It is where we plant our roots, fostering growth and nurturing our connections with others. It is a reminder that our journey is not just about reaching a destination but embracing the path with those we cherish.

Love, in its myriad forms, is the lifeblood of our souls. It enriches us, fueling our passions and softening our hardships. Through love, we find strength and resilience, allowing us to weather life's storms and celebrate its joys.

Being loved in return fills our hearts with warmth and validation. This reassurance shows us that others see and value us, reinforcing our self-worth. This reciprocal affection creates a network of support, reminding us we are never truly alone.

Last, having something to believe in gives us hope and motivation. Whether it is faith, a personal mission, or a dream yet to be realized, beliefs propel us forward, guiding our actions and decisions. They inspire us to strive for greatness and persevere in the face of adversity.

May these elements guide you as they have guided me, leading you toward a life of fulfillment, connection, and joy. Remember, the tapestry of life is woven not by solitary threads but by the intricate interplay of these profound truths.

Eye of the Beholder

When I was a child, one of my greatest delights was to witness Polaroid pictures come to life before my very eyes. After what felt like an eternity, the colors and forms within the frame crystallized into clarity, revealing the full image. It was a photograph birthed from the gaze of the beholder. Reflecting on those moments fills me with a sense of wonder.

Today, advancements have transformed the magic of photography. Since the dawn of the Polaroid, we have soared beyond our wildest dreams. Computers have grown from room-sized behemoths filled with intricate machinery to tiny chips that fit on the tip of a finger, holding a thousandfold the information and brilliance. Yet, the human mind struggles to keep pace with the ever-expanding complexities of our world. Where, I wonder, will these profound shifts lead us?

In her illuminating work, *Bird by Bird*, Anne Lamott shares, "One of the gifts of being a writer is that it gives you an excuse to do things, to go places, and to explore." She further muses, "Writing motivates you to look closely at life, at life as it lurches by and tramps around," offering a captivating perspective on the craft.

The great Flannery O'Connor once remarked, "Anyone who survived childhood has enough to write for the rest of his or her life." I count myself among those who continually seek fresh stories, using the compass of my personal history to guide my pen.

As a writer, I have journeyed through various roles—serving as a correspondent, columnist, and photographer for numerous newspapers. I have composed, recorded, and published hundreds of songs, along with volumes of poetry and prose. Among my subjects have been remarkable individuals, from former Vice President Al Gore to local heroes, all of whom have enriched my understanding of the human experience. Their tales of triumph over adversity have left an indelible mark on my soul.

Throughout the latter half of the twentieth century and into the dawn of the twenty-first, I have dedicated myself to capturing the essence of life through keen observation and reflection. The world around me captivates my senses, and while others may overlook its wonders, I feel compelled to share the stories that shape my existence.

From my earliest memories, I savored the myriad scents, sounds, voices, and hues surrounding me. My world was vibrant and full of energy. Where others saw only a forest, I discerned individual trees, spotted a red-tailed hawk perched high in the branches, and caught sight of a fox squirrel darting between them. A mockingbird, having just completed a graceful flight, landed with elegance on a nearby limb. Writing about these wondrous moments has always brought me immense joy. Music whispers along every pathway through the woods, glens, and valleys, with life pulsating all around me.

I have inhaled the earthy fragrances of the forest, traced my fingers over the rough bark of trees, listened intently to the calls of crows, and watched them take flight. The kaleidoscope of colors created by the morning sun filtering through the canopy enchants my very spirit, rendering me speechless. The gentle light of the setting sun, like a soothing balm, calms my soul. I leave no detail unexamined or overlooked. While some may deem these observations trivial, they occupy my thoughts throughout the day.

My wife revels in historical fiction and romance novels purely for entertainment, while I find personal and intellectual growth through my reading. I strive to understand the roles that each character plays in the grand tapestry of life, often underlining significant passages and words. My profound appreciation for the written word serves as a guiding light in my journey. The maps left behind by those who came before me illuminate my path, compelling me to carry the torch for those who will follow.

Henry Ward Beecher once stated, "All words are pegs to hang ideas on," and I wholeheartedly agree. I have dedicated my life's work to precisely achieving that. Words envelop me, infusing me with vibrant ideas and perceptions. The flow of concepts weaves together until they form a unified narrative, leading us to the heart of our tales.

Amidst the cacophony of voices filled with worry, condemnation, and despair, there is a more profound abundance of joy, contentment, and stability. Everyone craves a platform, yet while many voices resonate, others remain unheard.

As a writer, it is my duty to understand both people and the world that envelops them. I approach this calling with deep compassion for the role I play. Robert Stone captures it well when he says that writing is about "seeing people suffer and finding some meaning." This is the essence of the writing journey. I engage in conversation, focusing my attention on the vibrant life around me. A dear friend once remarked that I was never in the company of strangers, and he is right. If the signpost stands still, I will converse with it! I strike up dialogues to brighten the day of a young woman in distress at a medical facility or to offer encouragement to a cashier in a convenience store.

People are the heartbeat of my existence. Wherever I roam, I encounter a rich tapestry of humanity. Each person has a story to share, yet often others are uninterested in listening. Loving others more than they deserved was the right path. This understanding of genuine kindness has the power to transform adversaries into allies. I hold dear the saying, "Friends are people you haven't met yet." It is folly to let the world's unkindness and cruelty prevent us from connecting with others. There are many souls in need of tender loving care (TLC).

Johann Wolfgang von Goethe wisely observed, "Someone has already thought all truly wise thoughts thousands of times," but to make them truly our own, we must reflect on them until they take root in our personal experience. Thus, what I write reflects my understanding of life, the world, and my journey. While my experiences may not be extraordinary, they have been undeniably fascinating. Whether they are wise is up for debate.

Berthold Auerbach once said, "Only he is free who cultivates his own thoughts and strives without fear doing justice to them." I have endeavored to follow this wisdom, and each day reveals the genuine beauty of this world through the eyes of the beholder.

My journey has been one of constant discovery, a continuous dance between the familiar and the unknown. Every encounter, every word exchanged, and every fleeting moment captured through the lens of my camera, or the ink of my pen, adds another layer to the tapestry of my life.

It is this ever-evolving mosaic that I strive to understand and articulate, weaving threads of human experience into narratives that resonate with authenticity and empathy.

In this pursuit, I am ever mindful of the delicate balance between observing and experiencing. I aim to be present in each moment, allowing the stories of the world to unfold around me, while simultaneously seeking the deeper truths that lie beneath the surface. It is in these moments of quiet reflection that I find clarity and purpose, allowing me to translate the complex symphony of life into words that echo with sincerity.

A writer's journey is not solitary. Each person I meet and each story I hear is a thread that connects us all, creating a vast network of shared experiences and emotions. It is this interconnectedness that fuels my passion for storytelling, compelling me to explore the myriad ways in which our lives intersect and influence one another.

As I continue to navigate the ever-changing landscape of the modern world, I remain committed to capturing the beauty and complexity of life through my writing. Whether through the lens of a camera or the stroke of a pen, I strive to illuminate the nuances of the human experience, offering a glimpse into the hearts and minds of those I encounter along the way.

In this endeavor, I am guided by the belief that every story, no matter how insignificant, holds the potential to inspire, to heal, and to connect. It is this belief that drives me forward, encouraging me to embrace the wonder and mystery of life with open eyes and an open heart. And so, I continue to write, to explore, and to share the stories that shape our world, always hoping they will resonate with those who read them and, in some small way, enrich their own journey.

BRUSH STROKES

John Ruskin once mused, "Nature is painting for us, day after day, pictures of infinite beauty." Just as a Polaroid captures a fleeting scene, so too does an artist wield their brush to immortalize visions seen or imagined. Bob Ross, the beloved figure from television, declared, "I could create any kind of world that I wanted. Nothing hurts here, no pain, nobody is unhappy; it is a pleasant place. Everything is nice here." His joyous spirit resonated with all who watched him, his philosophy a vibrant tapestry woven from happiness and contentment. I fondly recall the moments spent watching him on television, playing with his pet squirrel, and feeling a wave of joy wash over me.

Saturdays were a ritual, as I tuned into PBS to witness Ross transform a blank white canvas into a breathtaking work of art in mere moments. It was pure magic! Within thirty minutes, a flowing green meadow or a majestic mountain scene emerged, crafted by his skilled hands. I marveled at his innate talent, amazed his brush danced across the canvas, conjuring images that had once existed only in his mind. He would cheerfully suggest, "Let's put a happy little cloud up here in the sky" or "Let's make this a grand old tree."

Years ago, I was fortunate enough to wander through the Louvre in Paris and the Prado Museum in Madrid, where some of the world's most cherished masterpieces reside. In the Louvre, I meandered through halls, searching for the famed *Mona Lisa* by Leonardo da Vinci, passing many illustrious works along the way. Finally, as I turned a corner, there it was, encased in glass against the wall. I found it smaller than I had envisioned, yet art connoisseurs have long revered it as a timeless treasure.

In Madrid, I stood in awe before the floor-to-ceiling masterpieces of Velázquez, the surreal wonders of Salvador Dalí, and the profound works of Pablo Picasso. It felt as though I had entered a grand cathedral, with the divine presence enveloping me. The thrill of witnessing such monumental paintings was exhilarating.

I limited my artistic endeavors to two years of high school art classes, where I learned the basics of color mixing and sketching. I passed both classes with an A, though everyone did! I realized two years of art class does not an artist make; I concluded that true artistry requires a gift I lacked.

However, a few years ago, Renee embarked on her own artistic journey and discovered her ability to paint. Our home is now adorned with her creations, though she humbly asserts she is *not* an artist. Yet, many—including myself—would heartily disagree. Artists often downplay their talents, but if her paintings grace every wall of our home, surely they possess merit.

Frank Stella once remarked, "One learns about painting by looking at and imitating other painters." Renee has drawn inspiration from Kevin Hill, a talented landscape painter from Clarksville, Tennessee. I accompanied her to Clarksville, where she took classes in the hotel's basement, thrilled at the opportunity. She completed three stunning paintings during our visit.

Renee often completes an entire eighteen-by-twenty-four canvas in a single day! I watch in admiration as each brushstroke breathes life into her creations. She seldom feels satisfied with the outcome, often exclaiming, "That's the best I can do." I respond, "That's far better than what I could do!"

Jean-Pierre de Caussade wisely stated, "We must offer ourselves to God like a clean, smooth canvas and not worry ourselves about what God may choose to paint on it, but at each moment, feel only the stroke of His brush."

This quote resonates deeply, reminding me that our lives are like "clean, smooth canvasses," eagerly awaiting the touch of the Master's hand. Each day presents a fresh start, a blank canvas upon which we can create our own masterpiece. Through God's grace, we possess the power to transform our lives into something beautiful with every stroke of His brush.

Just as Renee meticulously mixes her paints to achieve the perfect hue, we take what we are given and navigate each new day, weaving a vibrant tapestry of life. When the Master has finished painting our lives, I pray He will step back, look upon His work, and say, "Well done; I've done the best that I could do!"

Max Lucado, a cherished Christian writer, captures the essence of what I've sought to convey: "We serve as canvases for His (God's) brush stroke, papers for His pen, soil for His seeds, glimpses of His image."

Indeed, the brushstrokes of the Master Artist adorn the canvas of our lives. Every moment, every choice we make adds another layer, another color to our personal masterpiece. Just as Renee finds joy in her creations, so can we find joy in the unique art that is our life. Whether through the vibrant colors of happiness or the more muted tones of challenges, each stroke contributes to the richness and depth of our life's painting.

In the end, it's not about perfection but about the journey of creation. Like Renee, who bravely experiments with different techniques and styles, we too can embrace the beauty of experimentation in our lives. Each step forward, each new experience, is a chance to add to the story that only we can tell.

The act of painting, much like living, is a testament to the resilience of the human spirit. It's the courage to start with a blank canvas and transform it into something uniquely ours. As we continue to paint the story of our lives, let us remember to appreciate each moment, each brushstroke, knowing they are all integral to the masterpiece we are creating.

In this way, may we find fulfillment and joy, confident knowing that every day we can add beauty to the world, one brushstroke at a time.

Excessive Happiness

I guess I have been happy most of my life. Sure, there have been many difficulties, but I have survived most of them. I have given the Lord credit for bringing me through those times more than once. He has never let me down.

Happiness is a matter of choice, or at least that is the way I view it. People can choose to be happy or sad, discouraged, or victorious. My father used to tell me we make our own beds and must lie in them.

I saw a sign on someone's desk one day that said, "Life is like a coin: you can choose how to spend it, but you can never get it back." There is a lot of truth in that statement. Once we live our life, we spend it and cannot get it back. It is important we get it right the first time around.

I find my happiness in waking each morning next to my dear wife, Renee, who has endured my mannerisms and quirks for over fifty years. God bless her soul for having to live with me! She deserves a star in her crown when she meets her master one day.

My happiness also comes with that first cup of coffee in the morning. It is a treat for me and gets my day started with a bang. I also find happiness with my children and grandchildren. They have brought my life more joy and happiness than I deserve. I have often said that our grandchildren always look better in the rearview mirror, but I have only been kidding. They are all part of my joy and happiness.

I have found happiness in my work as an ordained minister for the past fifty-two years. From church to church, I have been blessed by some of the most wonderful, loving, and kind people who have supported me and the ministry to which I have been called. What a life! It has not been <u>work</u> for me at all, but pure pleasure.

And then there is my dog, Sassy. Before we got her, we had another dog named Blackie, and she was a joy to have around. Sassy has now become my best friend, my playmate, my confidant, and so much more. Renee thinks I am obsessed with her. Maybe so, but what fun we share when we go riding in "Daddy's truck." Pablo Casals said it best: "The capacity to care is the thing that gives life its deepest meaning and significance."

People have asked me: How do I find my yellow brick road? I always respond, "You're standing on it!" It is the very ground we walk on each day and how we view life and the things we encounter.

I have heard others say, "If only I could win the lottery!" or "Maybe one day my dream will come true." People who have yet to find genuine joy in their lives make both statements. Your happiness should never depend on whether you win the lottery or are waiting for your dream to come true or not. We find it in the here and now of life.

I have said so many times that whenever my ship comes in, I will be at the airport! Wouldn't that be something? And so, I do not depend on some magical ship to come in but live each day to its fullest with those around me who love and support me.

I like what David O. McKay said: "True happiness comes only by making others happy." You know, he was on to something there. When we make others happy, we become happy as well. It is a reciprocal thing.

A quote from Buddha states, "There is no path to happiness. Happiness is the path." Even Aristotle said, "Happiness depends upon ourselves." To show happiness to others, we must be happy ourselves.

Abraham Lincoln said, "Most folks are as happy as they make up their minds to be." We each have the choice to be happy. The Beatle John Lennon declared, "Life happens when you're busy making other plans." These are accurate words. If we enjoy what we are doing, then happiness will come to us during our task.

An old Chinese proverb states, "If you want happiness for an hour—take a nap. If you want happiness for a day—go fishing. If you want happiness for a year—inherit a fortune. If you want happiness for a lifetime—help someone else."

Eleanor Roosevelt said, "Since you get more joy out of giving to others, put a lot of thought into the happiness that you can give." We usually receive a lot more than we give. That is one key to giving.

Reverend Joel Osteen says, "Wake up every morning with a thankful attitude. Expect something good to happen in your life today." Believe that something good is coming your way, and even if it does not, your attitude will be positive. Be the change in your life today. On a poster, I saw these words, "Be happy... not because everything is good, but because you can see the good in everything."

In that wonderful movie, *The Bucket List*, Morgan Freeman and Jack Nicholson perch atop an Egyptian pyramid, and Freeman tells Nicholson about the requirements for entering Egyptian heaven. There were only two requirements for entry: (1) "Have you found joy in your life?" and (2) "Have you given joy to others?" The rich hospital owner and entrepreneur, Nicholson, has trouble with both questions. He has a daughter whom he has not seen in many years because of an argument they once had. His life has been one of taking from people and not giving back, so he miserably cannot answer either question. So many people spend their entire lives taking and never giving. You find joy in the eyes of your children, grandchildren, or loved ones. Nicholson's life had hardly affected any other person for the good, including his daughter or the granddaughter he would later discover. His life had been a miserable existence until Freeman confronted him about it and made suggestions about how he could correct the wrongs of the past.

Another movie that comes to mind is *Patch Adams.* Patch, played by Robin Williams, was in a mental institution at the beginning because he felt the need for help in his life. To help others, he checks out and attends medical school. He eventually falls in love with a classmate and works as an intern in the local hospital, where he enters a children's ward. To cheer the kids up, he donned a clown costume, complete with a big red nose, one day. He becomes an instant hit with the kids, who love his visits. The nurses on the ward are also very appreciative of Patch's actions toward the kids. But his medical supervisor is unsympathetic for his actions and asks him several times to stop being a child and begin acting like an adult doctor. Patch does not comply and continues to become an agent of good to those hurting and suffering children.

Near the end of the movie, the supervisor brings Patch before the counsel of his peers and charges him with "excessive happiness." Patch uses this to launch into a discussion of how doctors have become cold and unresponsive to the needs of their patients and how a little bit of laughter and happiness could touch the lives of those in need, if only used. After a vote, the school reinstated Patch and allowed him to graduate with his class.

The Gesundheit Institute, founded by Patch Adams as a charitable organization to provide healthcare services to the underserved, marks its fifty-first year of operation today. Established as an outreach program for the impoverished and those seeking to improve their well-being and mental state, the institute offers free medical care for those unable to afford it. Patch Adams, alongside a dedicated team of medical professionals and volunteers, has extended the institute's reach to various parts of the world, delivering essential healthcare services to those in need.

Nestled on a serene mountain in rural West Virginia, The Gesundheit Institute serves as a beacon of hope for individuals seeking compassionate and holistic medical care. The institute's philosophy revolves around the belief that healing should encompass not only physical health but also emotional and mental well-being. To learn more about The Gesundheit Institute and its impactful work, visit their website at https://www.patchadams.org.

Patch Adams's inspiring journey exemplifies the transformative power of spreading joy and kindness through healthcare. By leveraging his "excessive happiness" to aid others, Adams has positively affected the lives of thousands, embodying the institute's core values of empathy and altruism. As we commemorate this milestone anniversary, let's remember the profound impact one person's dedication and compassion can have on the world. In the spirit of Patch Adams, let us strive to spread happiness and wellness wherever we go. Remember, "Don't worry. Be happy!"

LEARNING THE HARDEST LESSONS

"I can't walk any further. I would like to go home!" Tom lamented; his spirit weary after merely two hours on the Appalachian Trail. He had cast aside his backpack, perched upon a large rock, resolutely declaring that he would not continue.

As his scoutmaster, I urged Tom to keep pace with the other nine scouts, for eight more miles lay ahead before we could rest at our first camp.

"But my feet hurt," he protested, anguish evident in his voice. "I've got blisters on my toes."

I explained to him that retreating to Amicalola Falls, where our five-day adventure began, would require a two-hour trek, with no one waiting to whisk him home, a five-hour journey away.

"But I can't go any further!" he cried in despair.

The other scouts had pressed on, leaving me behind, tasked with igniting Tom's motivation to move forward. I faced one of the hardest decisions of my life. I told Tom that I needed to catch up with the others, lest they wander off the trail. If he chose not to follow, I would have to leave him behind. I believed the prospect of solitude would spur him to action. Any parent can understand the heartbreaking choice I had to make for the sake of the entire troop, not just Tom.

Tom, much like many children today, struggled with motivation and resilience. Despite weeks of training focused on walking techniques and backpack essentials, he consistently lagged, offering excuses. From the start, he worried us on this journey, and his struggles became apparent on the first day. His parents had hoped this expedition would inspire him to break free from his shell.

In our preparatory weeks, we had ascended an old fire tower to strengthen the boys' ankles for our five-day hike. Most were between fourteen and sixteen, proving their endurance for such an endeavor. I expected some resistance from Tom, but not this early in our venture.

Leaving Tom behind on that rock filled me with dread, yet I knew sometimes tough love is essential to teaching perseverance. And so, I left him there, nibbling on a pack of crackers, hoping he would eventually choose to follow us, aware there was truly nowhere else for him to go. At fourteen, I believed he would grasp the message. I prayed fervently that he would rejoin us during one of our many breaks.

As night fell and the other scouts set up camp, Tom emerged, disheveled, fatigued, and worn to the bone. The others, frustrated, ignored him. I embraced Tom, offering encouragement and gratitude for his efforts to catch up.

"Tom, are you alright?" I inquired.

"Yes, sir. I thought I heard a bear after you left, so I started running. I soon ran out of steam but kept going."

In his solitary journey through the vast woods, Tom unearthed a newfound strength and resolve, reaching camp.

"I'm sorry for causing so much trouble, sir. I promise I will keep up from now on," he declared earnestly.

From that moment on, Tom transformed, often leading the pack, and outpacing the troop. I wouldn't quite label him a model Scout, but he certainly improved in various aspects of hiking, such as map reading and team spirit, and his attitude blossomed.

Was it fear that propelled Tom to catch up, or did something deeper within him awaken? Was it an instinct to fight or flee? Such mysteries remained unspoken between us.

Sir Edmund Hillary, the first man to conquer Mount Everest, once said, "It is not the mountain we conquer, but ourselves." Fifty years later, I remain convinced that Tom overcame his greatest fears that day. He learned an invaluable lesson about pushing beyond his limits. As the great Scot William Barclay noted, "Endurance is not just the ability to bear a hard thing, but to turn it into glory." That day, Tom discovered his own glory and would carry that experience with him for a lifetime.

Years later, I received a letter postmarked from Philadelphia, signed by Dr. Thomas Johnson. I had long forgotten

Tom's surname and hadn't seen him in nearly forty-nine years. But it was indeed my Tom. As I read his heartfelt letter, tears streamed down my cheeks when he expressed how the Appalachian Trail trip had transformed his life! He recounted his successes in high school and college, attending medical school to become a physician. It was hard to reconcile this accomplished man with the boy who had once sat crying on that rock.

Beverly Sills wisely stated, "There are no shortcuts to any place worth going." Many have attempted to hike the Appalachian Trail and faltered, as it demands perseverance, stamina, and an unwavering will. Anything of value in life requires effort, endurance, and the determination to achieve it. This young man had fought his way through medical school and was now making life-and-death decisions in a surgical suite in Philadelphia!

"Dr. Cravey," Tom continued in his letter, "I would love to thank you for taking me on that trip all those years ago. It changed my life. I will never forget that experience. I've even taken my children for a few walks on the trail, and they love it."

Mahatma Gandhi said, "Strength does not come from physical capacity. It comes from an indomitable will." Tom had found that indomitable will while perched on a rock in the wilderness forty-nine years ago. I am grateful to have played a small part in his journey of self-discovery and growth.

The Appalachian Trail stretches 2,200 miles across fourteen states along the Eastern Seaboard, from Springer Mountain, Georgia, to Mount Katahdin, Maine. Many aspiring hikers embark on this daunting journey, only to learn it requires more stamina and will than they expected. A saying among seasoned Appalachian Trail hikers rings true: "No pain, no rain, no Maine." Without the ability to endure pain or the rain, one cannot hope to reach Maine.

My dear friend Wayne McDaniel, and his granddaughter endeavored to complete this challenging journey a few years ago. She had just graduated from college and was eager to attempt the trail. Wayne, my contemporary, recognized his physical limitations, but agreed to accompany her. Before beginning their trek from Maine to Georgia, they climbed Mount Katahdin, which Wayne described as an arduous feat, yet he succeeded.

Prior to their journey, they stopped at a store where Wayne indulged in a prepared sandwich. He later felt something amiss and pressed onward, determined to continue with his granddaughter by his side. The forty-mile wilderness is one of the most challenging segments of the Appalachian Trail.

Two days into their adventure, Wayne fell gravely ill, attributing it to the sandwich. In desperation, his granddaughter hiked back to the ranger station for help. A helicopter airlifted Wayne to a local hospital for necessary care, abruptly ending their journey.

When our children were eight and twelve, my wife Renee and I embarked on a cross-country trip to the Grand Canyon in Arizona. The children cherished the experience, just as I did. I braved the descent down the Bright Angel Trail to the mighty Colorado River. A park ranger had informed me it would take about six hours, so we set off early the next morning with two bags of Sugar Babies and a canteen of water. Initially, I had considered a donkey ride down but discovered it required over a year of reservations! So, we hiked instead.

The Grand Canyon plunges one mile deep at the visitor's center. Reaching the river via the Bright Angel Trail demands navigating canyon walls and colossal boulders. Renee opted to stay behind and read while the children and I ventured forth. The morning sky was clear and beautiful, but the weather would soon shift by afternoon. We fed chipmunks some Sugar Babies, ensuring we conserved enough for ourselves during the hike. Soon, we realized the ranger had misled us! It would take much longer than six hours to complete the round trip. The journey to the river took four hours, and the uphill return awaited us.

The rain drenched us by the time we reached the summit. Renee was furious with me but supportive of the kids. I struggled to live that decision down, and I still find it difficult to this day. The trek demanded every ounce of strength we possessed, yet the experience was invaluable. How many children could say they had hiked the Bright Angel Trail and made it back?

Throughout life, from birth to death, we face challenges. Some may break us, while others strengthen us, but all contribute to our character, resilience, and the ability to learn life's toughest lessons.

Whether it's the winding paths of the Appalachian Trail or the steep descent into the Grand Canyon, these journeys teach us more than just the physical landscapes we navigate—they reveal the landscapes within ourselves. Each step taken in the face of adversity becomes a testament to our capacity for growth and transformation.

Reflecting on these experiences, we realize that the true value lies not in the destination but in the journey itself. It is about the moments of doubt turned into determination; the fears conquered by courage, and the friendships forged through shared trials. These are the stories we carry forward, the lessons we pass down, and the memories we cherish.

So, whether you're embarking on a literal trail or navigating the metaphorical paths of life, remember that every challenge is an opportunity to discover your own strength. It's about finding that indomitable will within, much like Tom did all those years ago, and knowing that every step, no matter how difficult, is a step towards becoming who you are.

In sharing these stories, may they serve as a reminder that the hardest lessons often lead to the most rewarding transformations. Let them inspire you to embrace the unknown, to push beyond your perceived limits, and to find glory in the journey itself. After all, the most significant journeys are those that lead us to discover the depths of our own potential and the heights of what we can achieve.

THE SONG REMEMBERS WHEN

It was a sweltering July afternoon in McRae, Georgia, where I found refuge on our back porch beneath the soothing shade of a tree, tuning in to the whispers of AM radio. In those days, central heating and air were mere dreams, so any respite from the sun was a cherished gift. The memory dances vividly in my mind. Suddenly, the disc jockey's voice crackled through the airwaves, announcing a song by a fresh talent from Macon, Georgia—just seventy miles away. My attention piqued as the haunting melodies of Otis Redding enveloped me. "Sitting on the Dock of the Bay" played, casting a spell that left me utterly mesmerized. At just fifteen, while strumming in a rock band and keenly following the latest musical stars, I recalled my brief stint at that very radio station, relishing the joy of spinning records from its rich collection.

In an instant, a wave of recognition washed over me—I knew Otis Redding. Each summer, I had visited him and some of his family while spending weeks with my first cousin, Danny. Otis too was a musician, mingling with legends like Little Richard Pennyman, the Allman Brothers, and Gladys Knight and the Pips, all of whom would gather on the streets of Macon, their laughter and music spilling from porches as bands practiced nearby. The sixties were an electrifying era in Macon, brimming with artistic fervor.

Otis was soaring in the music world, the Allman Brothers were igniting excitement on their tours, Gladys Knight and the Pips were captivating hearts with soulful rhythms, and Little Richard was the pride of the town. Macon was truly a vibrant sanctuary for music and the arts, blossoming with each passing day.

When I first heard Otis's song, I knew it would always stay in my memory—songs possess that enchanting power to connect us to moments and experiences that enhance our lives, even during challenging times. I recalled the days when Renee and I were dating, spinning old eight-track tapes of the Bee Gees and John Denver, their melodies forever linked to those sweet memories.

At thirteen, I implored my mother to impart the secrets of chords and notes on her guitar, and thus began my lifelong journey with music. That very year, I played in my first rock band, tasting success within our local realm.

Music has always been the heartbeat of my existence. I have strummed in rock bands, sang in gospel quartets, and harmonized in choirs. My two years in high school chorus saw me performing baritone in a men's quartet that placed second in the state during my final year.

Since I was thirteen, I have written songs for numerous groups and soloists, weaving music into the very fabric of my life. I have recorded seventeen personal albums of religious music, several of which graced the airwaves.

One of the most thrilling moments was when I composed a fight song for my beloved alma mater, Georgia Southern University, in Statesboro, Georgia. Attending a football game with my wife that year, I heard it played in full orchestration during halftime—a moment of pure joy as she pointed it out, for I had never experienced my piece brought to life by a university band.

As many of you know, composers craft music within time signatures, such as 4/4 time. Once you grasp its rhythm, you realize each measure holds four beats, with each quarter note receiving its due. Rests, too, play a crucial role, holding their own time value, even if silently.

Count Basie once mused, "It's the notes you don't hear that matter." Imagine a world devoid of rests; the music would lose its luster. Much like impressionistic art, where vibrant colors paint beautiful scenes yet remain elusive until pointed out, music conceals its rests, waiting to be discovered.

Can I say more? Music is a profound language, speaking to each of us in unique ways. There exists a mystical allure to it, a mesmerizing force. Truly, the song remembers when.

As I sit here reflecting on those cherished memories, I realize how deeply music has intertwined with the tapestry of my life. Each melody, each lyric, holds a fragment of my journey, a reminder of who I was and who I have become. It's as if the songs themselves are time capsules, preserving emotions and moments that might otherwise fade with the passage of time.

The power of music lies in its ability to transcend boundaries, to connect us to one another and to our past. It is a universal language that speaks to the heart, resonates with shared experiences of joy, sorrow, love, and hope. The songs we hold dear are not just mere notes and words; they are the soundtrack of our lives, echoing the stories that define us.

As I continue to create and share music, I am filled with gratitude for the gift it has been in my life. I hope that, through my melodies, I can offer others the same solace and inspiration that music has always provided for me. In this way, the song will always remember when, carrying forward the legacy of those unforgettable moments that shape our souls.

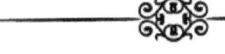

JUSTIFICATION

A Christian Perspective

Do you recall when you first felt the spark of intellect surpassing that of your parents? And what about the adventurous spirit that ignited your first act of defiance against authority? Reflect on the ultimate repercussions that followed your youthful rebellion. While I may shy away from revealing my own consequences, I suspect we all share these formative challenges as we traverse the landscape of growing up.

In the sacred text of Genesis 12, we witness God's command to Abram, urging him to gather his belongings and embark on a profound journey. Accompanied only by Sarah, his beloved wife, and Lot, his dear nephew, Abram is beckoned towards the mysterious land of Canaan, an uncharted territory. Consider this: Abram was 75 years old! While many of his peers basked in leisurely retirements in sunny havens like Panama City or Cancun, Abram was called to start anew. Imagine the swirling emotions within him! I, for one, would feel a tinge of hesitation to embrace such a daunting command, yet Abram remained steadfast in his faith, ready to rise to the challenge—a readiness we too must cultivate when the Lord calls upon us.

As I pen these words, it is the second Sunday of the sacred forty-day journey of Lent, leading us to the celebration of Easter. This season invites us to relinquish certain comforts to focus intently on our relationship with Christ. How many souls are choosing to forgo distractions that impede their spiritual paths? What have you chosen to surrender? We show our devotion to God by giving up the things that stand between us and His grace. If we find ourselves uncertain of God's calling, it may be because our schedules are too cluttered to hear His whispers.

The tale of Abram resonates with both a profound lesson and a divine promise. It speaks to the challenge of leaving behind the snug cocoon of familiarity and stepping boldly into the unknown, guided solely by faith. In this journey,

Abram recognizes that his earthly attachments must yield to the embrace of divine grace. Abram must forsake sin, let go of all idols, and depart with only his closest loved ones.

In return for his obedience, God bestows upon Abram six promises:

1. I will transform you into a great nation.

2. I will bless you abundantly.

3. I will elevate your name; Abram would become Abraham, his identity forever changed.

4. You will become a source of blessing.

5. I will bless those who bless you and curse those who curse you.

6. Through you, all the nations of the earth shall be blessed.

Would we heed such a call? At God's behest, would we abandon the comforts of home and family to venture into foreign lands or new horizons? True rest eludes us until we respond to God's call with unwavering faithfulness. He yearns for intimate fellowship with us, inviting us to trust Him. To achieve this, we must relinquish our own agendas and embrace Christ.

Let us turn our attention to Psalm 121, where David beautifully assures us that the Lord will bless and protect us in all our endeavors if we remain obedient to His call. He will protect our comings and goings.

In Romans 4:1-5 and 13-17, Paul explains the doctrine of justification by faith, using Abraham as a prime example. He asserts Abraham believed *in God, and it was reckoned to him as righteousness.* The Jews held tightly to the laws of God but often dismissed Paul's teachings on faith alone. Paul clarifies that faith naturally leads to action and adherence to the law, with promises granted to Abraham through faith, not mere adherence to the Law.

In John 3:1–17, we encounter Nicodemus, a devoted Pharisee and member of the Sanhedrin, who approaches Jesus under the cover of night, seeking answers. Recognizing Jesus as a revered teacher, he questions the possibility of being born again. How could one re-enter their mother's womb? Jesus replies, "What is born of the flesh is flesh, and what is born of the Spirit is spirit" (KJV).

Nicodemus struggles to see beyond the Old Testament laws, hindered by his belief in "works."

Jesus then reveals the essence of salvation to Nicodemus in verse 16: "For God so loved the world that he gave his only begotten Son, that whosoever believeth in him should not perish but have everlasting life." This profound simplicity might have been too much for Nicodemus, leading him to retreat into the shadows.

The core message unfolds:

1. God is calling forth new Abrahams into our world.

2. God promises to bless our obedience.

3. We rest assured in His protective embrace.

4. Justification comes through faith in Jesus Christ, believing in Him personally and responding to His call.

> 5. Finally, we must experience rebirth through water (Holy Baptism) and the Spirit.

If you hear the divine call beckoning you today, I invite you to approach His throne of grace. Should you feel your faith wavering, come, and lay aside that which may obstruct your deeper connection with the Lord. If your spirit hungers, nourish yourself. If you yearn for a new beginning, step forth in faith and surrender your heart entirely to Christ. Leave behind the law and embrace justification through your faith in the Almighty. Christ extends this invitation. Come. Embrace this moment of divine invitation with an open heart, for it is a chance to embark on your own journey of transformation. Just as Abram heeded God's call for courage and faith, so, too, are we encouraged to rise above our fears and doubts, trusting that the path laid before us is guided by His wisdom and love.

In these sacred times of reflection and renewal, let us ponder the legacy we aim to leave, inspired by the promises made to Abraham. As we navigate the complexities of our modern world, may we find solace in the timeless truth that faith, not mere adherence to rules, is the key to a life aligned with God's will.

The journey of faith is not without its challenges, but it is also rich with blessings and opportunities for growth. By choosing to walk this path, we open ourselves to the transformative power of God's love, which can change not only our own lives but also the lives of those we touch.

So take this moment to listen deeply, to discern the gentle whisper of God's call in your life. Whether it leads you to acts of kindness, moments of introspection, or bold steps into the unknown, know that a divine promise that transcends time and space supports you. May grace, purpose, and a deepening connection to the One who calls us all by name fill your journey.

I Saw God in the Muck and Mire

I beheld the Divine gliding across the shimmering expanse of Lake Pontchartrain, a miraculous sight emerging from the tempest of Katrina's wrath. He stood at the threshold of a ravaged, waterlogged abode, waving gently to those who passed, yet their eyes, unseeing of His grace, sought not His presence.

I witnessed Him tenderly embrace a weary soul, returning home after three long months, only to find her sanctuary in utter disarray. With a gentle touch, He, through the hands of devoted volunteer church members, reached her heart. These humble souls of faith, emerging from an old church van, strove to restore what the chaos had lost. Her tears flowed freely, a silent testament to God's enduring presence.

The waters surged to five feet high, submerging her sanctuary, erasing a lifetime of cherished memories—photos, clothes, toys, certificates, and beloved tomes. Her pain resonated deeply, and in that poignant moment, God's heart ached alongside hers, bearing yet another cross, mending another heart, longing to reconcile a fractured world.

Through it all, I saw God and clasped His hand, journeying together through the mire of shattered dreams and life's trials. Where were you?

"There but for the grace of God..."

That mission trip continues to resonate deeply within my heart, vividly reminding me of humanity's resilience and the boundless grace found amidst devastation. As we labored under the oppressive heat, each nail driven and wall rebuilt became a testament to the power of community and faith.

For every home reclaimed from the ruins, there was a story of hope rekindled, a family reunited, and a future reimagined. The laughter of children returning to their neighborhoods and the grateful smiles of parents offered glimpses of redemption, as if the very streets themselves were healing from the scars of disaster.

In those moments, I understood the Divine does not live solely in grand cathedrals or distant heavens, but walks among us in the kindness of strangers, in the shared burdens of neighbors, and in the unwavering spirit of a city determined to rise again. As we packed up our tools and bid farewell to the people of New Orleans, I knew that our collaborative work created a song that would resonate long after the last hammer fell silent—a melody of love, resilience, and divine presence echoing through the ages.

(Written by Dr. Cravey during a mission trip to New Orleans, Louisiana, as his team toiled in disaster relief under the sweltering sun.)

SHEEP AND SHEPHERDS

Psalm 23

I have always found myself enchanted by the gentle nature of sheep and the steadfast courage of shepherds, who undertake one of the most demanding of tasks. Thus, I felt compelled to revisit both these creatures and the sacred bond they share.

Having grown up amidst pigs, chickens, and cows in the heart of South Georgia, I was a stranger to sheep until adulthood. In many lands, these woolly beings serve as a primary source of sustenance, forming a bond with their shepherds that is as unique as it is profound. David, in the beloved Psalm 23, beautifully articulated this relationship, illustrating how the shepherd mirrors our connection to God, the ultimate shepherd of humankind.

Sheep are heedless, often neglecting their own well-being. They wander aimlessly in fields, risking separation from their flock, and may find themselves ensnared in rugged rocks or teetering perilously over cliffs, blissfully unaware of the looming dangers. It is the shepherd's sacred duty to nurture and protect them, a role that demands unwavering commitment.

In the New Testament, Jesus proclaims himself the Good Shepherd (John 10:11 KJV), who cares for his flock, even to the point of sacrificing his life for them. As we delve into Psalm 23, each verse unveils a tapestry of spiritual inspiration.

Verse 1 establishes the divine hierarchy: God reigns supreme, and we are but sheep in His pasture, requiring guidance. "The Lord is my Shepherd; I shall not want." David, speaking as a humble lamb, acknowledges God as the ultimate Creator and Master of His flock. His ownership of us ensures He meets our needs, and we will never genuinely want.

Human desires often stretch into an endless array: a new car, lottery winnings, an ideal partner, beautiful offspring, a fulfilling job, or a charming home. Yet, these are not our genuine needs! God, in His infinite wisdom, knows precisely what we require and provides accordingly.

Verse 2 reassures us of God's omnipotence, guiding us to lush pastures for nourishment and serene waters for refreshment, understanding our timid nature that shies from turbulent streams. He expects our needs and fulfills them with grace.

In Verse 3, we see God as the restorer of our weary souls, gently guiding us back into His embrace when we stray, leading us along the paths of righteousness, and grounding us on solid footing.

Verse 4 encourages us to cast aside fear of lurking threats or the "shadow of death," for God walks beside us through every trial. His promise never to forsake us is a beacon of hope. The shepherd's rod and staff provide comfort; the rod directs and disciplines, while the staff, with its gentle curve, rescues wayward sheep from harm.

In Verse 5, we learn that God preemptively surveys new pastures, ensuring no poisonous weeds threaten His flock. He clears the way, preparing a feast for us in safety.

The phrase "anoints my head with oil" symbolizes the care a shepherd provides to soothe the sheep's wounds, guarding against summer's pests and allowing them to graze freely in the autumn.

Finally, in Verse 6, the writer speaks of the "goodness and mercy" of God that follows him relentlessly, regardless of circumstance. God's grace and kindness are unwavering, ensuring His children are never devoid of comfort. The verse also hints at the eternal dwelling He has prepared for us, assuring, "I will dwell in the house of the Lord forever."

As we return daily to the verdant pastures God provides, may we find solace in knowing that we are His, and He is ours. Those who wander outside His will face constant peril and anxiety.

What a beautiful narrative of our bond with God and our enduring response to His love! This passage remains one of the most cherished and frequently read in the scriptures.

It serves as a timeless reminder of the depth of divine love and protection, painted vividly through the imagery of sheep and their shepherd. This relationship transcends time and culture, offering comfort and guidance through life's complexities.

Reflecting on these verses invites us to embrace a life of trust and faith, acknowledging that, like sheep, we are often unaware of the surrounding dangers. Yet, we have a Shepherd who blesses us, knows our hearts, and paths, and walks with us, providing solace and strength.

This understanding encourages us to live with gratitude and awareness of our spiritual journey, constantly guided by His wisdom. As we meditate on the words of Psalm 23, may we find peace in the assurance of divine presence, knowing that no matter where we roam, the Shepherd's love and guidance are ever-present, leading us toward green pastures and still waters.

May this reflection deepen our appreciation of the sacred relationship between humanity and the divine and inspire us to walk steadfastly in the light of faith, ever mindful of the Shepherd who holds us in His care.

PERSONAL THOUGHTS

One's wealth or popularity, or educational status does not bring about happiness in this world. It is in knowing oneself and having someone to love and someone to love you that makes the difference and allows you to live a life with meaning and purpose.

—Charles E. Cravey

THE MAINE THING

A delightful Maine vacation rewarded Renee and me for our dedicated years managing Statesboro condominiums. Weeks in advance, and with eager hearts, we carefully prepared for our trip, ensuring everything was in order. Our journey would begin with a gathering of fellow travelers in Savannah, Georgia, and span seven days aboard a luxurious bus, weaving through the states of Georgia and Maine. Our destination, Booth Bay Harbor on Maine's southern coast, filled us with anticipation, particularly the thought of savoring freshly caught Maine lobster accompanied by all the delightful fixings.

On the morning of our grand adventure, we set forth early. By seven thirty, we were en route, joined by approximately forty kindred spirits. Both retired and ready for a leisurely exploration of the coast, we embraced the promise of adventure.

Our first stop was a charming lunch in South Carolina, followed by an evening in Virginia, where we mingled with our fellow travelers over a delightful meal. We retired early that night, eager for the adventures that awaited us tomorrow, including a stop in New Jersey, right across from the iconic skyline of New York City.

The next day brought us a ferry ride to the Statue of Liberty, followed by a brief but soul-stirring walk on Liberty Island. The air hummed with history as we approached Ellis Island, the sacred ground where many of our ancestors first set foot in this land of opportunity. Nostalgia and excitement filled our hearts at the thought of traversing the same halls where they once filled out their papers.

As we journeyed through the bustling streets of New York City, gazing at the towering skyline from the interstate, we pressed on toward Booth Bay. After refreshing ourselves that evening, we enjoyed a special lobster feast at a nearby restaurant. A knowledgeable server guided us through the intricate art of lobster dining, revealing the secrets of cracking and savoring the delicacy. However, Renee had been experiencing discomfort in her upper abdomen throughout the trip, which cast a shadow over our culinary enjoyment.

That night brought her little rest, her pain persistent as the stars twinkled above. The following morning, after breakfast, we embarked on a harbor boat tour, though Renee's discomfort lingered. Eventually, she confided in me her intention to visit a local clinic with the tour director. There, after examining x-rays and conducting tests, the physician diagnosed her with pancreatitis and recommended transport to the nearest hospital, thirty miles away.

Panic washed over me as I grappled with the unfamiliarity of our surroundings. With our tour group scheduled to depart early the next morning, I sought the tour host's assistance to rent a compact car, determined to be by Renee's side. I navigated the winding roads to Damariscotta, a quaint town with a charming river, quickly finding the hospital where the compassionate staff guided me to Renee's room.

In her distress, Renee lamented the disruption of our trip, but I reassured her that all would be well. I had arranged for a place to stay nearby until her recovery. That evening,

I returned to our motel, my mind heavy with thoughts of her well-being, as I strolled along the dock, the water reflecting the muted glow of the moon.

The next morning, as the tour group prepared to board the bus, each member offered heartfelt condolences, expressing their prayers for Renee and our family. I thanked them, knowing their journey to West Point awaited, while mine lay in ensuring Renee's recovery.

Once the bus had departed, I returned to the hospital, spending the day by her side. Her condition had improved, and she encouraged me to explore the sights. Despite my desire to be with her, I ventured on a lighthouse tour, yet the experience felt incomplete without her companionship. My thoughts centered on how we would return to Savannah after her discharge.

As the days passed, Renee's health steadily improved, and by Friday, the physician expressed hope for her discharge around noon. True to their word, we received the green light to leave that afternoon. With her cellphone, Renee arranged our flights from Portland, Maine, to Atlanta, and onward to Savannah, where our vehicle awaited.

We journeyed from Damariscotta to Portland seamlessly, returning the rental car just in time for our flight to Atlanta. The trip was uneventful, but the turbulence during our last leg to Savannah felt like a tempestuous dance; we were relieved when we finally landed close to midnight.

We took a waiting taxi to the motel where our car was parked. However, Renee's renewed pain marred our hour-long drive back to Statesboro, prompting her readmission to our local hospital that Monday for further treatment.

What a whirlwind of events! Our expected getaway had transformed into an unforeseen saga, yet we remained grateful it wasn't worse. Since that fateful trip to Maine, Renee has faced additional hospital visits, though none has been as tumultuous. Throughout our ordeal, we reminded ourselves, "The main thing is to make the Maine thing the main thing." In those moments, nothing else mattered but her recovery.

Note: Our foresight in purchasing trip insurance for $200 turned out to be a blessing, as the company reimbursed us for our airfare, meals, and other incurred expenses. With the refund, we embarked on a few quick trips, grateful for the grace that allowed us to heal and move forward. All praise and thanksgiving be to God, who makes everything possible and mends our souls. Our journey to Maine, though fraught with unexpected challenges, taught us the importance of resilience and the value of togetherness in times of adversity. Despite the initial disappointment, the experience reinforced our appreciation for life's unpredictability and the strength we draw from our loved ones.

Back in Statesboro, our daily routines resumed, but we carried with us the memories of our journey and the lessons learned. Renee's health gradually stabilized, and we found solace in the support of our community, who welcomed us back with open arms.

As we reflected on the trip, we realized that the true adventure lay not in the destinations we visited, but in the shared moments of laughter, worry, and relief. Each obstacle we encountered only strengthened our bond, reminding us that life's most treasured moments often arise from the most unexpected circumstances.

In the months that followed, we often spoke of returning to Maine, this time under more favorable conditions, to explore its beauty with renewed gratitude. Until then, we cherished the stories we gathered, knowing that our journey was far more than a mere vacation—it was a testament to love, perseverance, and the unwavering human spirit.

As we continued to navigate life's unpredictable paths, we kept the Maine mantra close to our hearts: making the main thing the main thing, focusing on what truly matters—health, happiness, and the joy of shared experiences.

"Just Aren't Enough Rocks!"

During my younger years, I was fortunate enough to visit Israel and explore the Holy Land. This experience was truly a blessing—informative and unforgettable. It marked the beginning of three trips, with this one being the most memorable.

While our tour group was in Jerusalem on that first trip, our guide halted our progress on the Via Dolorosa, also known as the Way of the Cross, because of a significant disturbance ahead. We had no choice but to wait until the local police resolved the situation. After some investigation, we learned that two groups of local teenagers were in a heated confrontation, throwing stones at one another from across the street. The officers we spoke to noted that the area frequently experiences such conflicts, emphasizing the historical use of stones as weapons.

Looking back to biblical times provides insight into how divisions first arose and the reasons for conflict. In the book of Genesis, we read about Adam and Eve's first two sons, Cain and Abel. Out of jealousy and greed, Cain killed Abel in a field. Cain, the firstborn after Adam and Eve, set a troubling precedent. Later in Genesis, we encounter the story of Jacob and Esau, twin sons of Isaac and Rebekah, who struggled even before birth (Genesis 25:21–26). This was just the beginning of stone-throwing; Esau famously traded his birthright for a bowl of stew!

Historians acknowledge Jacob and Esau as the patriarchs of their respective nations. God renamed Jacob as Israel, revealing that he would lead twelve tribes. In contrast, Esau's descendants, referred to as Edomites in Genesis 36, did not enjoy the same favor from God. For a time, Israel and Edom were adversaries.

God held them accountable for their actions, resulting in consequences. It's no surprise that people throw stones; the Holy Bible contains numerous examples of such behavior. However, the methods we use to solve problems are a different matter entirely.

In my early elementary school years, I was a mischievous child frequently sent to the principal's office. I have mixed memories of that time. One day during recess, students were disruptive and throwing rocks across the playground, which contributed to my troubles. I carelessly broke a school window, leading to severe consequences.

That evening, my parents disciplined me, adding to the punishment I received from the principal. I quickly understood that I couldn't satisfy my anger by throwing rocks. This was a lesson I learned early on.

My parents were strict disciplinarians, often resorting to physical punishment. Their misguided understanding of discipline led to frequent beatings, leaving us all bruised. I sometimes tried to evade their punishment. If this happened today, authorities might charge them with child cruelty, but in the 1950s, people considered it normal, resulting in much rock throwing.

At thirteen, after lashing out, I broke into a building and the police arrested me; I spent time in the county jail. One could blame me, my parents, or my upbringing, but peer acceptance was challenging.

My father's alcoholism exacerbated our volatile situation. When he was angry, my mother often endured his aggression, and I felt compelled to defend her.

When my father was calm, he wasn't abusive. However, our family's struggles made a poor impression on our surroundings.

Many children today live in conditions similar to or worse than mine. Psychiatrists warn that these marginalized children may grow into troubled adults, filling our jails and psychiatric wards if left without support. They cannot throw enough stones to ease their anxiety, frustration, and feelings of inadequacy. Without guidance in coping with their circumstances, the prognosis is grim. Many will struggle to meet societal expectations and mature into capable adults without significant help. Their pain will linger, exacerbating their circumstances. Their children may endure similar harsh forms of discipline that I did, perpetuating a cycle of suffering.

Throughout my mission work, I have traveled to countries with extreme living conditions. In some Third World nations, people live in dire poverty, often uncertain of when their next meal will arrive. During my trips to León, Nicaragua, I witnessed appalling living conditions in a small town in the volcanic mountains. At a modest school with around seventy-five children, teachers prepared basic meals using methane gas sourced from a pit where banana peels and trash decomposed. This precarious cooking method posed a constant explosion of risk.

Our mission team would bring aid to families known as the "dump people" who lived nearby in an area where towns dumped their trash. Each visit was a heartbreaking experience.

Hundreds of individuals lived in makeshift cardboard homes constructed from refuse. Their tattered clothing carried a foul odor. Yet, we brought food to prepare on an open grill and served them alongside meat and condiments. They were grateful, allowing us to share Holy Communion after the meal. We would hug the children before leaving, providing them with boxes of clothing.

I always departed, feeling an urge to throw rocks at the injustice of their conditions.

Atrocities fill the world in places unknown to many, where people suffer profoundly every day and lack necessities like food and water.

A dear friend of mine, Bobby Gale, accompanied me on a mission trip to Costa Rica and became passionate about mission work. He has dedicated years to digging wells in Ugandan villages lacking clean water. Before the wells, many suffered from waterborne diseases, resulting in numerous deaths. Bobby, though just one person, demonstrates the impact one individual can make. He collects contributions from various churches, establishing more wells with the small donations. His dedication to this ministry is remarkable, and hundreds of volunteers have joined his efforts. "There, but for the grace of God go you and I."

Bobby is slowing down now, and I often wonder who will carry on this essential work after him.

In one of my favorite films, *Forrest Gump* (1994), Ginny, Forrest's childhood friend, grows up in an abusive household on the outskirts of town. The dilapidated house stands amid a cotton field. One day, as they walk down a dirt path, Ginny picks up rocks and hurls them at her old home. Exhausted, she falls to her knees. Forrest kneels beside her and states, "Sometimes, I guess there just aren't enough rocks."

After leaving home in the 1960s, Ginny immerses herself in a world of rock-n-roll, drugs, and a transient lifestyle, drifting across the U.S. with various groups of hippies. Near the movie's conclusion, she returns home and marries Forrest, living in the family home where he grew up. The memories of her painful experiences in that house haunt her. Forrest understands that throwing rocks will never heal her internal wounds, as the house is merely an object. Rocks cannot erase her suffering. "Sometimes I guess there just aren't enough rocks."

Many people today resonate with Ginny's story. They have endured much pain, and regardless of how many rocks they throw, they cannot erase their past. They carry scars, striving each day for better outcomes.

"Sometimes I guess there just aren't enough rocks."T his poignant metaphor captures the futility of trying to ease deep-seated pain with surface-level actions. Instead of throwing rocks, which only offers a fleeting sense of release, individuals need compassion, understanding, and tangible support to truly heal. The journey to overcome past traumas is often long and arduous, requiring patience and empathy from both the individual and those around them.

In addressing these challenges, it's crucial to foster environments where people feel safe to express their emotions and seek help. Community support systems, mental health resources, and open dialogues about personal struggles can pave the way for healing and growth. By acknowledging the struggles of others and offering a helping hand, we can break the cycle of pain and create a world where healing is possible for everyone.

As we reflect on these stories, whether from personal experiences or those we've witnessed, we're reminded of the power of kindness and resilience. Each minor act of compassion can be a stepping stone towards a better future, not just for oneself but for entire communities. It's about building bridges, not walls, and understanding that sometimes, it's not about the rocks at all, but about the love and support that surrounds us.

A Majestic Encounter

As soon as my son reached the age where my wife granted her approval for him to accompany me on fishing adventures, I took him to the enchanting ponds and lakes of our locale. This cherished tradition has flourished for over thirty-five years, filling our hearts with joy as we cast our lines together.

One memorable occasion found us nestled in a cozy cabin in the North Georgia mountains, alongside the mighty Toccoa River. Our intention was to embrace the art of fly-fishing, yet my heart belonged to my trusty Zebco rod and reel, adorned with live bait. The world of fly fishing felt like an elusive enchantment, so I entrusted that endeavor to my son.

On this early morning, as the sun's golden rays filtered through the verdant canopy embracing the river, Jonathan waded upstream, embracing his fly-fishing gear. I settled downstream, near a gentle stretch of water, when suddenly, a captivating sight caught my eye. A majestic bald eagle soared from the stream before me, clutching a shimmering rainbow trout in its talons! Awe washed over me as I beheld the eagle gliding downstream with its glistening catch. My son, drawn by the commotion, hurried to my side. I exclaimed in wonder that a bald eagle had just snatched the very trout I had almost caught! He chuckled, aware that large fish seldom graced my line, and together we marveled at the spectacle. Such moments of wonder are rare in a lifetime, and I felt truly privileged to witness that breathtaking scene.

Equally magnificent is the time spent with my only son. His demanding work often keeps him away, making each fishing trip a precious connection. I hold on to the hope that, in the years to come, he will treasure the adventures we shared. Though my back troubles me now, I strive to make these outings memorable for him.

Reflecting on the wisdom of former President Jimmy Carter, a son of Plains, Georgia, he once remarked, "Many of the most publicized events of my presidency are not nearly as memorable or significant in my life as fishing with my dad." Even now, at ninety-eight years old and facing health challenges, the memories of fishing with his father gleam among his life's highlights, outshining discussions with kings and humanitarian endeavors.

Harry Middleton wisely noted, "Fishing is not an escape from life, but often a deeper immersion into it." There's magic in sitting beside a bank or afloat in a boat, casting your line into the shimmering waters, each hope for the catch of the day igniting a thrill in the heart of any child.

Doug Larson's words resonate deeply: "If people concentrated on the really important things in life, there'd be a shortage of fishing poles." Indeed, the moments I cherish most have revolved around fishing. My two brothers and I joyfully fished with simple cane poles throughout my childhood. Our adventures to nearby creeks and ponds often rewarded us with a bountiful catch. My eldest brother, Raymond, possessed an innate talent for fishing; he could sense where the fish lingered. Before he died, Raymond took me on countless fishing trips, and I'll always cherish those memories, filling the void left by my hardworking father.

Henry David Thoreau, the great naturalist, once declared, "Many men go fishing all of their lives without knowing that it is not fish they are after." His words suggest that the veritable treasure lies in nature's embrace, in the beauty that breaks the monotony of life. Engaging with the elements while fishing is a remedy for the spirit, and catching fish is but a delightful bonus!

Had I not ventured into the North Georgia wilderness with my son on that fateful day, I would have missed the breathtaking sight of the bald eagle soaring with its prize. What a majestic encounter it was! The next adventure awaits just around the river's bend.

I am ever grateful for these shared moments, for they are the threads that weave the tapestry of our lives together. Each trip is a reminder that the essence of fishing is not merely in the catch's pursuit, but in the shared laughter, the muted contemplation, and the stories that become legends in our family lore.

As we prepare for our next journey, I cherish the anticipation—the early morning chill; the mist rising from the water; and the promise of what the day may bring. The river is a teacher, imparting lessons in patience, perseverance, and humility, and I find solace in its timeless flow. With every cast, I am reminded of the bonds that tie generations, and if I can hold a rod, I will continue this cherished tradition with my son.

May the rivers we fish always mirror the love and connection we share, and may the memories of these adventures stay with us long after we make the last cast. Here's to the magic of fishing and the joy of being in nature's embrace—a treasure beyond measure I hope my son will carry with him, passing it down to the next generation.

The Master's Cut

I had needed a haircut for several weeks, and Renee finally convinced me to go to a barber. We had just moved that week to a new appointment in a larger city where I would be the pastor of a large intercity church. Renee wanted me to look my best on my first Sunday before a new congregation, so I took off in search of the perfect barbershop.

A few miles from the parsonage, I found a shop, parked, and walked in. I signed in and sat down with a few men ahead of me, so I figured it would be a long wait. As I looked around the shop, I saw three barbers. Two of them looked to be in their thirties, but the guy at the back was gray-haired and looked to be around eighty years old. *Just my luck*, I thought. *I will get the old guy in the draw.*

I watched man after man get up and move to an available chair. My time was nearing, so I held my breath and watched for the next available chair. Sure enough, the old man's chair became available, and he called for me by saying, "Next!"

I made my way to the back of the shop where the old man's chair was and sat down, and he began talking. In fact, he was talking nonstop! I just wanted a haircut and to skip all the formalities, but he was incessant. After wrapping my neck with the usual cloth and pulling my shirt back a bit, he grabbed his instrument and began slowly and methodically clipping my long hair. Then it began. He asked me who I was and what I was doing in Macon, Georgia. I told him I had just moved to town to pastor a certain church and needed a barber.

"Son, you came to the master!" he stated. "I have a lot of good friends in that church, and I cut their hair regularly."

We shared a lot of pleasantries as he cut. He then picked up his electric razor, placed a clip on it, and cut some more.

"Where are you from, son?" he asked. I told him, and he then said, "You know, I rode home on the Greyhound bus from Fort Bragg, North Carolina, with a man from McRae. His name was Carise."

I told him it had to have been my father. He was the only man I had ever known with that name.

He then asked, "Is your last name Cravey?"

"Yes, sir."

The aging man then unraveled a tale about that trip on the bus and his meeting with my father. "He and I sat beside each other all the way to Macon and shared a lot of things. I really liked the guy, and we promised to stay in touch, but we never did. You know, time, jobs, living in towns so far apart. We never really got around to meeting again, but I remember him well."

He talked then about his military service and the fact he had cut hair at several bases in Europe and in the States before mustering out of the military. He shared things my father had shared with him I had never known before. I soon became enthralled with this fellow and his talk.

As he began trimming my beard, he asked if I was a veteran, so I shared my experience with trying to join the Navy while back in college and having to go to Atlanta for my induction preliminaries. There, they put me through a battery of exercises and tests, but I failed the color test, discovering I was colorblind, and the military labeled me 4-F. They send 4-F people home, calling them up only if another war starts. I was thankful for the designation, for I felt that my father had given enough service to the nation without me having to go.

The elderly barber said he understood and was thankful I did not have to witness the atrocities he and my father had seen. "Your father shared with me twice where he came so close to a bullet that he could hear it whiz by his ears. You should thank your father that you did not have to go."

"My father died in 1966," I responded. "He was only fifty years old and died of a hematoma to the frontal lobe of his brain. My brothers, mother, and I struggled afterward, but we got by."

"I am so sorry, son, for your great loss. I am certain you miss him." As he finished his work, he spun me around in the chair so I could see myself and my haircut in the large mirror on the wall. "That's the master's cut," he exclaimed. "If I never see you again, we will always have this bond between us with your father. God rest his soul."

I would have never envisioned such an exquisite haircut. Indeed, it marked the beginning of many transformations given by the master barber. Just a couple of years later, fate took a cruel turn as he succumbed to a formidable stroke, leaving me heartbroken when I returned to the barbershop days later, only to learn of his passing. The following day, I stood beneath an umbrella, drenched by the downpour, at his graveside funeral while the pastor delivered the eulogy. As the military performed the solemn twenty-one-gun salute and carefully folded the flag atop his casket, I found myself enveloped in more than just the rain; tears cascaded down my cheeks as I reminisced about this cherished soul and his serendipitous encounter with my father. My father's service resonated profoundly with the essence of my barber's.

I will forever cherish the memory of my time in the master barber's chair. It's astonishing to think that, at first, I had yearned for one of the younger barbers. Just imagine the treasure I would have forfeited had I not chosen to sit in the master's embrace!

In the years that followed, I often reflected on the wisdom and stories shared by the elderly barber. His gentle hands and kind words had left an indelible mark on my life, reminding me of the profound connections we can form with others, even in the most unexpected places.

Every time I glimpsed myself in the mirror, I remembered not only the haircut but also the lessons learned and the legacy of my father and the barber—two men who had lived through times of great challenge and remained steadfast in their dedication to others.

In my new role as pastor, I drew inspiration from their stories, sharing them with my congregation to illustrate the power of kindness, resilience, and the unexpected bonds that can shape our lives. It was a testament to the enduring influence of those we meet along our journey and how their impact can ripple through time, touching not just our lives but those we lead as well.

Whenever I felt the weight of my responsibilities or faced challenges, I would think of the barber's words and the warmth of his presence, and it would bring me solace. It was a reminder that, like him, I too could make a difference in someone's life, one conversation at a time.

THE FIRST DAY OF THE REST OF MY LIFE

The dawn of the first day of the rest of my life emerged nine years ago, heralded by an unexpected heart attack. In retrospect, I can vividly recall enduring a prolonged and intense storm of stress that enveloped me for nearly two years. On that fateful day, I found myself hunched over in my recliner, consumed by an overwhelming sensation that felt as if my chest might burst forth. The agony was excruciating.

Two long years passed before a stress test and subsequent heart catheterization revealed the truth of my heart attack. The discovery unveiled a patch of scar tissue gracing the front of my heart, a clear sign of my past ordeal. The catheterization further uncovered a constriction in the lower right coronary artery. To combat my high blood pressure, my doctor prescribed Coreg, along with Plavix, a blood thinner, and a baby aspirin. My doctor informed me that stress primarily caused heart attacks and advised me to eliminate unnecessary stressors from my life. That marked the inception of the first day of the rest of my life, a journey I now eagerly expect.

Heeding my doctor's counsel, I embarked on a quest to de-stress my existence, shedding the burdens that weighed me down. For my survival, this arduous yet vital task became imperative.

Certain strains of stress cannot simply vanish overnight; they demand daily diligence to combat the underlying factors at play. Each individual faces unique challenges, and it is crucial to discern these elements and gain the skills necessary to navigate them effectively.

After four decades devoted to the ministry within the United Methodist Church, I realized it was time to retire my robes and explore new passions. The moment I made this choice, I felt an immense weight lift from my shoulders. In the months leading to my retirement at the annual conference, my excitement grew for the opportunities that lay ahead. Had I remained in full-time ministry, I would have missed the countless experiences now available to me. Retirement would grant me the precious gift of training my two grandchildren, Meghan and Benjamin, spending cherished moments with them. I could embark on extended adventures with my dear friend Terry and his wife, expanding my horizons. Even as I devoted time to mission work, I could still seize opportunities to preach whenever fate allowed.

Gradually, my stress diminished. The most significant source of it would soon fade into the past. I resolved to embrace a new life, one that blended the wisdom of my experiences with the thrill of new interests. My household chores, lovingly dubbed the honey-do list, would flourish, making way for my passions to take center stage. I had finally broken free from the chains that had held me captive for so long. The remaining years were now mine to savor.

And so, I find myself here, celebrating the first day of the rest of my life. It is a delightful and transformative shift in perspective. I am filled with gratitude for the chance to rediscover joy and fulfillment in ways I hadn't imagined before. Each day is now a canvas, ready to be painted with experiences that enrich my soul and bring me closer to those I love.

As I delve deeper into this new chapter, I have embraced hobbies that once seemed like distant dreams. Gardening has become a therapeutic ritual, where the simple act of nurturing plants mirrors my journey of self-care and growth. In the quiet of my backyard, I find peace and a connection to nature that rejuvenates my spirit.

Travel, too, has become a newfound passion. Whether exploring the quaint charm of nearby towns or venturing to distant lands, each journey is an adventure that broadens my perspective and fills my heart with stories to cherish. The world is vast and beautiful, and I intend to savor every corner.

I have rekindled my love for music, picking up the guitar I had long set aside. Strumming its strings and weaving melodies has been both challenging and rewarding, a reminder that learning never truly ends. Music speaks to the unspoken parts of my being, and through it, I find a voice that is both familiar and new.

In this phase of my life, I am not merely living; I am thriving. Surrounded by family and friends, supported by the wisdom of experiences, I approach each day with curiosity and an open heart. The journey is far from over, and I eagerly embrace the unexpected turns that lie ahead.

Indeed, this is the first day of the rest of my life—a testament to the power of resilience, the beauty of change, and the promise of a future filled with hope and endless possibilities.

NOT JUST A CUP OF COFFEE

Coffee. Hot, black, and soothing coffee. Colombian, rich, strong, and awakening coffee. Roasted beans, lovingly harvested from the majestic mountains of Colombia, journey to my cup. The sun kisses each bean until it reaches its zenith of perfection. Laborers, with hands calloused by toil, gather the beans along misty hillsides beneath the nurturing embrace of puffy white clouds. Countless souls have conspired to bring me this delightful cup of morning Joe. As I sip in my cherished recliner, I am whisked away to those muddy hillsides of Colombia, Costa Rica, Nicaragua, Honduras, Guatemala, Ecuador, Venezuela, and Jamaica—lands where I have savored some of the finest brews of my life during mission trips. I will always remember the faces I encountered along the way. Each expedition has been a treasure, a tapestry of unforgettable experiences.

My morning Joe possesses an enchanting ability to renew these vivid memories, inscribed upon the pages of my life—indelible and irremovable. Such thoughts transport me to distant places and times, and I consider myself blessed to have these opportunities. Yet, my journey was not always so illuminated.

Before these adventures unfolded, I resisted every call to join a mission trip when friends or colleagues extended their invitations. Fearful of flying, I shunned the idea entirely. But in 1980, after persistent encouragement from a dear friend, my church rallied to raise funds for my journey to Costa Rica. They presented it to me one fateful morning, making my participation official. With a heart full of gratitude, I packed for the ten-day journey ahead.

In Costa Rica, our tasks involved mixing mortar, laying concrete blocks, and teaching local children in a VBS setting. We stayed in the southernmost town, a stone's throw from Panama. Our accommodations were humble, resembling a barracks with basic bunk beds. After a night spent battling mosquitoes, I awoke to a heavenly aroma wafting from the parsonage next door. Rising with the dawn, I ventured outside to find the pastor and his wife gathering coffee beans from a mound in their backyard. Engaging them in my limited Spanish, I followed them into their home to witness the grinding and brewing of the morning coffee for our team's breakfast. They offered me a cup, and it was pure bliss! Until that moment, I had never been a devoted coffee drinker, but that single cup transformed my perspective forever! It was simply divine!

Thus began my love affair with mission work. I would later lead teams to France and Spain and return to Costa Rica, traversing Central and South America. As either a team member or leader, I embarked on sixty-eight foreign missions, and after catastrophic events like hurricanes and tornadoes, I engaged in local mission trips across the States as well.

Following Hurricane Katrina, I led three recovery teams to New Orleans, mucking out and cleaning homes in flooded neighborhoods. During our first trip, just a week after the hurricane, FEMA granted us access to New Orleans for cleanup. On that initial day, our team of ten took a lunch break at the only open fast-food establishment—Popeyes.

While we ordered, a gracious woman approached our group and inquired about our purpose in town. Upon learning we were there for hurricane relief, she said, "As long as you folks are in New Orleans working, the meals here are free! Come by every day, and my staff will serve you without charge!" On the third day, I discovered she was the owner of all Popeyes restaurants across the United States—a truly remarkable and generous soul whose kindness I will never forget.

Breakfast in Costa Rica was a feast of fresh fruits, alongside the essential bacon and eggs, sourced from the very yard of the parsonage. Once again, another cup of Joe, and then another. The scene forever enchanted me.

To you, dear friend, it may simply be another cup of coffee, but to me, it is a treasure far beyond the ordinary. Each sip is a reminder of the connections forged through shared experiences and the simple acts of kindness encountered along the way. It's a testament to the resilience of communities and the power of the human spirit in times of need.

The aroma of coffee in the morning has become a ritual, a moment of reflection and gratitude for the journeys I've taken and the lives I've touched. It symbolizes the warmth and hospitality of the people I've met—the stories exchanged over steaming mugs and the friendships that blossomed amidst the clinking of cups.

As I sit here with my morning brew, I am reminded that coffee, like life, is a blend of flavors—a mix of the bitter and the sweet, the robust and the mild. It's a celebration of diversity and the coming together of unique elements to create something truly remarkable.

So, as the steam rises from my cup, I am filled with hope for the adventures yet to come and the stories still waiting to be written. Here's to the next cup of coffee and the journey it will inspire. Cheers!

Pot-Liquor Hill

Ah, those enchanted days of childhood, imbued with wonder! Though ages seem to have drifted by, the memories of my cherished haven remain vivid in my heart. We called it "Pot-Liquor Hill," a magical realm of my youth where I navigated the awkward formative years, gathering the hard-earned lessons that would guide me throughout life.

In the 1950s, Pot-Liquor Hill was a simple yet vibrant community just beyond the railroad tracks, thriving with small farms and exquisite flower gardens. Families stood united, ever neighborly, relying on one another in the tapestry of daily life. Most souls walked to their destinations, for cars were a rare luxury. I recall but one family on the Hill possessing a television, a black-and-white marvel, where we all gathered to mourn the tragic day of President John F. Kennedy's assassination and to witness his funeral.

It wasn't until I was around twelve that my father gifted us our own black-and-white TV, on which we watched the first steps upon the moon unfold in magical silence.

I delighted in shows like *Gunsmoke*, *Rin-Tin-Tin*, *Leave It to Beaver*, and *The Lone Ranger*, each episode weaving tales that captivated my imagination. One Christmas, I received an authentic replica of the Lone Ranger's guns, a treasure that crowned my young existence. For those fleeting years, I stood as the guardian of Pot-Liquor Hill, valiantly defending against imagined foes, despite my weapons being mere plastic.

Pot-Liquor, the savory essence released when turnips dance upon the stove, was our culinary delight, often enjoyed with crumbled cornbread. Yet, the Hill also whispered of other "liquors," illicit brews crafted from corn mash and secretive ingredients, sold in pint bottles from hidden corners. Those in the know kept their lips sealed to protect their kin from the watchful eyes of the law.

Giles' Grocery Store, nestled across the tracks at the base of the hill, was a treasure trove of wonders. With a quarter in hand, I could indulge in an ice-cold R.C. Cola, a chocolate moon pie, and a handful of Red Hots, still finding change to spare! We bought kerosene for our home heater from Giles', a more accessible choice than laboriously chopping wood.

Life on the Hill revolved around the turpentine still, where trucks would line up to deliver barrels of pine tar, transformed into resin through an intricate process filled with bubbling cauldrons. The steam rising over the nearby creek was a reminder of the labor that sustained many families.

During summer's embrace, they summoned boys like me to toil at truck farms, earning a handsome five dollars for a full day's labor harvesting watermelons, cantaloupes, cucumbers, and more under the relentless sun. Saturdays were the golden days of spending our hard-earned coins.

Nighttime brought another challenge as we caught chickens for local poultry farmers, a task fraught with difficulty and scratches from the feisty hens, yet rewarding in its own right as we earned five dollars for each night's work.

With our modest earnings, we always contributed to our family's grocery needs, knowing well the value of our garden's bounty. Pickling and canning became summer rituals, preserving our harvest for the cold winters ahead and ensuring our survival until the new crops arrived.

Back then, we lived by the creed, "If you don't work, you don't eat!" This ethos instilled in us a robust work ethic, a steadfast understanding of responsibility that shaped our lives, even when met with reluctance.

Calamities touched the Hill, yet the community's spirit shone brightly as families rallied to support one another in times of need. If a neighbor fell ill, we would gather vegetables, canned goods, and essentials, embodying the true essence of camaraderie. This was our local welfare, a time when people genuinely cared for one another, sharing all they had. How the tides of time have shifted, as many now seek government aid instead of the warm embrace of community support!

The world may have changed since those halcyon days on Pot-Liquor Hill, but the lessons we learned there remain timeless. Our simple joys and shared hardships knitted us together, creating bonds that could withstand any storm. I remember the laughter that echoed through our small community, the kind that came from deep within and washed away the day's troubles. It was the laughter of freedom, of knowing that we had each other, no matter what.

As the years passed, the hill saw fresh faces, and the landscape shifted with the march of progress. Yet, the essence of those early days lingered in the stories we told and the memories we cherished. Even now, as I stroll through the modern streets of my adult life, I can sometimes catch the faint scent of pine tar or hear the distant clatter of a train, and I'm transported back to that magical place where it all began.

Pot-Liquor Hill may not exist on any map, but it lives on in the hearts of those who called it home. Its spirit endures in the values we carry forward: hard work, resilience, and the enduring power of community. It reminds us that no matter how far we travel, the places and people that shaped us remain a part of who we are, guiding us on our journey through life.

FINDING GREG ALLMAN'S GRAVE

Rose Hill Cemetery, nestled in the enchanting town of Macon, Georgia, perches gracefully upon a steep hill that ascends from the gentle embrace of the mighty Ocmulgee River. With arched entrances beckoning from Riverside Drive, it invites visitors into a realm of eternal rest. For over two centuries, this sacred ground has welcomed the souls of notable figures, including a dedicated section for the valiant dead of the Civil War. Among its hallowed inhabitants lies Greg Allman, the renowned keyboardist of the legendary rock band, The Allman Brothers.

Two years following his passing, I wandered through the sprawling expanse of the cemetery in search of Greg's last resting place. My connection to Greg dates back over sixty years to my teenage summers spent in Macon with my cousin. Though not my home, it was a city where we roamed freely, exploring its pool halls and vibrant streets. On one such adventure, we crossed paths with Greg, his brother Duane, and their circle of friends. Poised to transform the musical landscape with their fiery Southern rock, the Allmans were still emerging from the shadows.

With a heart full of nostalgia, I yearned to pay my respects at Greg's grave, yet the vastness of the cemetery proved daunting. Armed knowing that it lay near the river, I set forth, but alas, my search bore no fruit.

Returning to the welcome center, I found it shuttered for lunch. Time was fleeting, as I had a two-hour journey back to Statesboro awaiting me. I departed with a sense of frustration and disappointment, yet a spark of determination ignited within—Greg wouldn't be going anywhere before my return!

Six months later, as fate would have it, Renee and I found ourselves back in Macon for a doctor's appointment. With renewed resolve, we ventured to Rose Hill once more, intent on discovering Greg Allman's resting place. We navigated the cemetery's narrow lanes, gazing upon headstones that told tales of lives once vibrantly lived—soldiers who fought bravely, famous figures, and ordinary souls alike.

After an hour of searching, we found ourselves still in pursuit of his grave. Once again, the welcome center was closed for lunch! But this time, I was undeterred. We patiently waited for it to reopen, and we received precise directions and a map to his burial site.

With newfound knowledge, we journeyed down the hill towards his resting place, which was nestled in a secluded cove that could easily be overlooked. A small parking area awaited just below, guiding us to park and embark on our ascent to the plot.

At last, we arrived at the fenced burial site of Greg, his brother Duane, and fellow band members Butch Trucks and Berry Oakley. Among them lay a grave marked with the name of Elizabeth Reed, a tribute to a musical composition featured on one of Allman's albums.

As Renee and I stood in reverence before these graves, memories of the simpler days of the 1960s washed over me—the carefree laughter and youthful escapades. I reminisced about the time I had even bested Greg in a game of Rook! Ordinary boys from Georgia, destined for extraordinary paths—while Greg and Duane achieved global fame, I found my calling in the ministry, preaching a different gospel.

To my surprise, I had envisioned a grand monument in Greg's honor, yet his grave was humble, unassuming. We are all mere mortals seeking our place in this vast world. And finally, I had discovered the resting place of Greg Allman. The moment was bittersweet, filled with a sense of completion and quiet reflection. Standing there, I felt a profound connection not just to Greg and the music that had been the soundtrack to so many lives, but to the city of Macon itself—a place that had nurtured not only the Allman Brothers but also countless other artists and dreamers.

As we lingered, a gentle breeze rustled the leaves of the towering oaks, creating a melody of its own, a fitting tribute to the musicians who lay beneath. It was as if the wind carried whispers of their songs, inviting us to remember not just their music, but the lives they had touched and the legacies they had left behind.

We spent a few more moments in muted contemplation, paying homage not just to the past, but also cherishing the present—the bonds of friendship, the power of music, and the memories that continue to shape us. As we walked back to the car, I knew that while our visit was complete, the spirit of the Allman Brothers would forever remain in the heart of Macon and in the music that continues to resonate through the decades.

Driving away from Rose Hill, I felt a sense of peace, knowing that I had finally fulfilled my journey. I had come seeking closure, and in doing so, I had found a deeper appreciation for the lives and stories that intertwine with our own. The road ahead seemed brighter, filled with the promise of new adventures, and a reminder that though time may pass, the echoes of the past are never truly far behind.

THE MIGHTY HIAWASSEE

Coursing through my memory

Like tales from long ago,

Its cool and rushing waters

Bring balm unto my soul.

I stand beside its mighty banks and cast a wishful eye.

And glimpse a passing eagle's flight

Which wings toward the eastern sky.

O'er rocks so ancient to this earth,

I watch its waters roll.

Cascading down to Murphy town,

Confluence of the soul.

Roll on, you ancient river,

Carry all my dreams away.

Renew them all tomorrow

As we start a brand-new day.

—Written on the banks of theHiawassee River near Brasstown, North Carolina, while on vacation

One Square at a Time

A few years ago, I enrolled in a creative writing class at Georgia Southern University, my cherished alma mater, to refine and elevate my writing craft. This enchanting experience unveiled how much I had "unlearned" since my university days, rekindling the pure joy of purposeful writing and the delight in savoring each word.

My instructor, a beacon of eloquence, was well-versed in contemporary writing techniques, yet she imparted timeless truths that resonate within the literary realm:

Who—What—Where—When—Why

Who took action? What was accomplished? Where did it unfold? When did it occur? Why did it transpire?

One exercise she introduced was delightful. She invited us to form a square with our fingers, using both hands, and then craft an essay about the wonders we perceived within that compact frame. Inch by inch, we dissected the elements within our view, describing each with intimate detail.

I focused on the television in the room, the stand that cradled it, and the myriad elements that surrounded it. As I wrote, I explored the virtues and vices of television today, reflecting on how society has grown since my youth. I even scrutinized the brand of the TV, pondering its stature among its peers. The sturdy oak stand beneath it inspired me to marvel at the beauty of its wood grain and the storied life of the two-hundred-year-old tree it once was, imagining the sapling that would take another two centuries to reach such grandeur!

At the close of our hour-long session, we submitted our reflections on the treasures we had encountered in our little square. To my surprise, I had penned six pages about the inanimate objects within my frame, while my classmates barely filled a page! My instructor, astonished, proclaimed, "You must be a writer." I chuckled and replied, "A would-be writer."

I encourage you to try this exercise yourself. Form a square with your fingers and record the details of what you see. Your perspective shifts may astound you. Enrich your observations and expand upon their significance in your life.

An artist engages in a similar creative process. They do not begin with every element of their masterpiece, but with one focal point, gradually layering the background and foreground until their vision stands complete.

Now, let us conjure a story together. I shall provide you with hints, and you can weave your own narrative around them.

WHO did it? Bonnie Carter (a name plucked from the ether)

WHAT did she do? She ventured to Belk's to find a new dress.

WHERE did she go? To downtown Columbus, Ohio, within the bustling confines of the Springer Mall Shopping Center. The day was alive with activity; people thronged everywhere, and the sky hung heavy with clouds, promising rain later.

WHEN did it happen? Last Thursday, after she concluded her workout at a gym just two blocks away, where she exercised three times a week.

WHY was she there? It had been ages since she had treated herself to clothing, and she felt the urge to indulge in a new dress, a rare splurge for herself.

At home, she juggled the needs of three children, often prioritizing their wardrobes. Expand upon this premise, letting your imagination soar! Perhaps:

A young man approached the desk clerk at Belk's, demanding cash from the register. In a sudden twist, someone pulled the fire alarm, sending shoppers rushing outside just as the rain poured in torrents, and she realized she had forgotten her umbrella. An elderly lady stumbled at the checkout, hitting her head, prompting a call for an ambulance.

The possibilities are endless, and your story will take shape as you explore. Remember, not every detail needs to be laid bare; allow certain elements to linger in the reader's imagination. As our instructor advised, "Show, but don't tell."

And there you have it—you've crafted your masterpiece! It matters not whether anyone else will ever read it; what counts is that you engaged in a positive and constructive exercise for your mind today. Consider keeping a journal of the sights and experiences you encounter.

My wife, the artist, has a treasure trove of oil paintings that only family and friends will ever admire. Yet, she finds profound joy in each creation, each canvas a masterpiece in my eyes, for I am not an artist.

I have amassed volumes of stories, poems, and musings as exercises to sharpen my intellect, enhance my research skills, and hone my craft. We must never relinquish our quest for life and creativity, whether in the art of writing, painting, or nurturing deeper connections with others.

Embrace the beauty of life, one square at a time! Each day, as you embark on this creative journey, you'll find new squares to explore and fresh stories to tell. Whether it's the quiet corner of your favorite cafe, the bustling energy of a city street, or the serene solitude of a forest path, every moment holds the potential for inspiration.

As you continue to practice, you'll discover that writing is not just about filling pages, but about capturing the essence of a moment, a feeling, or a fleeting thought. It's about connecting with your inner voice and allowing it to guide you to places you never imagined.

Remember, the world is your canvas, and your words are the brushstrokes that bring it to life. So, take a moment each day to pause, form that little square with your fingers, and delve into the wonders that await within. Let your imagination run wild and your creativity flourish.

In doing so, you not only enrich your own life but also contribute to the tapestry of stories that bind us all together. Each story, no matter how small, adds a unique thread to the fabric of human experience. So, go forth and create, for the world is waiting to hear your voice, one square at a time.

MY ROMANCE WITH PAPER

I have always cherished an enchanting romance with paper. The touch, the texture, and the intoxicating scent have captivated my senses throughout the years. It all began on that momentous first day of first grade when Mrs. Stephenson bestowed upon us our very first sheet of paper, adorned with letters and numbers awaiting our trace. In that magical moment, I forged a bond with the page and the art of writing. To me, numbers and letters transcended mere symbols; they became vessels of creativity, allowing me to weave narratives that conveyed my innermost feelings. In those formative days of youth, I envisioned tales taking shape, a means to express my heart's whispers. I could write about anything—scaling the heights of a mountain and capturing the awe of valleys below or the celestial expanse above, the thrill of soaring in my first jet, the exhilarating rush of my inaugural roller coaster ride, or my maiden voyage beyond Georgia's borders, discovering a world that mirrored my own. Writing has opened countless doors for me, and to think it all began with that singular sheet of paper in first grade!

Paper, a gift from the trees—primarily pine trees, of which the state of Georgia boasts abundant numbers. As a budding teen, I toiled alongside a pulpwood man during the two-week Christmas break. He and his crew would fell young pine trees, known as pulpwood, while I helped load them onto transport trucks. Those days were arduous for a twelve-year-old, yet the five-dollar reward at day's end made it all worthwhile. Sticky pine tar would ooze from the freshly cut trees, adorning my clothes, hands, and shoes, requiring kerosene or gasoline for a proper cleanse upon returning home.

From the forest, the trees journeyed to a paper mill, where they underwent a remarkable transformation—grinding and chipping until the pulp became a fine slurry. This concoction would be cooked, steamed, and extruded until it morphed into a "soup" ready for pressing into large sheets of paper, cut, wrapped, and dispatched to warehouses for distribution to stores and merchants. It is a wondrous process that allows us to cradle a single pristine sheet of writing paper in our hands. How precious that sheet truly is!

There lies immense power within the written page. Through discourse and treatises, people can alter the course of humanity, penning thoughts that impact our daily lives for better or worse. Consider the profound effects of the Holy Bible, the world's perennial bestseller, which has transformed millions of lives through its verses of poetry, prose, and timeless lessons. Reflect on the exquisite writings of Shakespeare and countless dreamers who have shaped our world, granting us glimpses into the intricacies of love and life.

I fondly recall my first visit to our school library in the first grade. I quickly became enamored with the scent of old books in that sacred haven. I devoured them, though initially I could only gaze at the illustrations, as I yet could not read. As the years passed, I would check out volumes, bringing them home to peruse repeatedly until their contents became imprinted in my memory.

Books became an integral part of my identity, gateways to fantastical realms or journeys around the globe, guided by captivating imagery. I felt as though I had unearthed an entirely new dimension of existence through the artistry bound within their pages.

And here I stand, authoring yet another book. Approaching the twilight of my life, I feel a calling to leave something tangible behind for the little ones who will traverse the libraries across the nation after me. They too may fall in love with the written word and learn to savor each phrase and sentiment. They might even become authors, sharing their own stories with us. And to think, it all begins with a single tree, bestowing life far beyond its own. Each tree is a precious gift from the divine. Indeed, I have a romance with paper! As I continue to pen this narrative, I am reminded of the symbiotic relationship between nature and creativity. The trees, with their steadfast presence, offer more than just the paper upon which stories are told; they provide the inspiration to imagine and create. Their rustling leaves echo the whispers of countless stories waiting to be discovered, as if urging us to listen and write.

In the quiet moments of reflection, I ponder the legacy I hope to leave. With each word I write, I aspire to kindle the flame of curiosity in young minds, encouraging them to explore the vast landscapes of their imagination. I envision a future where eager readers fill libraries, each discovering their own passion for storytelling.

Embracing this romance with paper, I am grateful for the timeless connection it forges between generations. It is a bridge that links the past, present, and future—a testament to the enduring power of words. As I conclude this chapter, I am filled with a sense of fulfillment, knowing that my love affair with paper will live on in the hearts of those who come after me, inspiring them to author their own stories and contribute to the ever-growing tapestry of human experience.

GRAVE NUMBER 291

A little white cross stands amid other white crosses in a row, silently overlooking the hillside we are standing on. It is cold and frigid as we prepare for the funeral with only a few people there: the prison warden, the cell block guard, two trustees, and me, the designated pastor. I would deliver a eulogy for someone I have never met. A six-foot earthen hole had been dug by a backhoe machine, which now sits motionless against the fence. A simple marker in front of the little countryside cemetery details the cemetery's founding and its first interments. Each cross has been pre-numbered, and there are no names upon them, no birthdates, or dates of death. Just a number!

As I stood and gazed into the open grave, ready for a burial today for number 291, I felt saddened by the anonymity of it all. A friend had explained that the cemetery was a pauper's cemetery for prisoners who had died at the state prison and had no family members to claim their bodies. Many of them had died from the AIDS epidemic, such as the guy I was about to bury. Those in charge had not even told me his name.

This was my fourth funeral in what the inmates referred to as "Piss Ant Hill" cemetery. Known for the little red ants that had infested the area, the cemetery had garnered terribly negative feelings from the inmates. This is where the state buries such remains.

As I stood and looked upon the cemetery with its faceless markers, I could not help but compare it with each of us and our situation. The Bible clearly reminds us we are all sinners saved only by the grace and mercy of Jesus Christ. We were all at one time outcasts, strangers, and pilgrims wandering in the wilderness of sin until we met the Savior and became new creatures in Him. Each of these prisoners was once babies in their mother's arms, cared for, loved, protected, and given sustenance. Now, they have become nobodies—not even one person to claim their bodies at death! This sad ending to a life with so much potential will soon see the prisoner forgotten, remembered only as number 291!

I delivered the customary eulogy, offered the familiar prayers from my prayer book, shared a few heartfelt closing remarks, and observed as the two trustees began the solemn task of lowering the casket. Scoop by scoop, they gently tossed dirt from the mound onto the casket until they finished their task. Once completed, guards escorted them back to the prison, a mere few hundred yards away.

As I stood there, the late evening air grew colder, yet it could never rival the chill that settled in my heart. An all-consuming emptiness enveloped me, a sensation I had known at each of these mournful gatherings. It is profoundly sad and heartbreaking. I can only hope and pray that their souls have found salvation. The wind whispered softly through the trees, carrying with it the unspoken stories of those who lay beneath the earth. I paused for a moment, reflecting on the fleeting nature of life and the enduring hope of redemption. Despite the somber reality of these unmarked graves, I held onto the belief that each life, no matter how forgotten, had touched the world.

Turning to leave, I glanced back at the row of crosses, silently vowing to remember them not just as numbers, but as individuals who once lived, dreamed, and sought connection. As I walked down the path leading away from the cemetery, I resolved to bring a little more light and compassion into the world, honoring those who could no longer do so themselves.

MUSES AND MEMORIES

To those who pass along knowledge to a young child, who makes a difference in their lives through teaching or sharing, who walks with us the "Road Less Traveled," we give heartfelt thanks. Without those muses, our lives would be completely different.

—Charles E. Cravey

Blackie's Arrival

She came to us like a gift from God. After having had dogs most of our married lives, Renee and I had sworn off having any more when our last one died about twelve years ago. Our grown children had left home to start their own lives, so we no longer felt obligated to have dogs. Dogs are wonderful creatures—do not get me wrong—and are so much comfort, but they are like children. One must keep them fed, play with them to keep them happy and content, take them to the vet regularly, and buy the medications they prescribe. It can get to be an expensive annual fee and is like having children. Renee and I are both retired and just felt that a dog would tie us down when we wanted to take a trip, not to mention the kennel fees that would accumulate. So, we were not looking for a dog.

Blackie showed up one day in our yard and had fleas and ticks all over her body, along with sandspurs she had picked up from wandering through the woods. We live in the country and have plenty of woods surrounding our property. She was a mess and needed attention. She was being chased by a pack of dogs and was in heat. I chased the pack of dogs away, and Blackie was appreciative, for she took up on our front porch and slept there for a few nights to come. She had no collar on, so we called the local <u>pound</u>, and they told us we could not keep her and had to bring her in. If, after seven days, no one claimed her, she would be ours if we wanted her. We just knew that someone would claim her because she was a solid black, beautiful Boykin Spaniel.

Seven days later, I called the pound, just hoping no one had claimed her. They told me she was ready to be picked up and the charge would be forty-five dollars! What? Forty-five dollars? What did I do wrong? They explained any dog brought in would have to have updated shots, and that was the fee.

After I had paid the fee, they brought her in, and her first sight of me was all she needed. She came running to me, jumped into my lap, and started licking my face and hands, so eager I had returned to get her. So, I loaded her into the car and drove home to announce to Renee that we had a dog! I was not so sure it would make her happy, but she was accepting of her.

I named her Blackie because she was solid black. A picture of her appears on the back cover of this book just for reference. She was friendly, and we could tell she had belonged to someone who had done a super job raising her. I built a doghouse and put it on our front porch, and she stayed in it for a couple of weeks until we decided that if we were to keep her, we would have her fixed so we would not have the problem of other area dogs chasing after her whenever she went into heat.

After that, we brought her in from outside, and she took to our laundry room simply fine and slept there each night. The vet had guesstimated she was about a year old, and she still had a lot of playful <u>puppy</u> left in her. She captured our hearts quickly, and we fell in love with her. She was, as Renee called her, the most perfect dog that had ever lived! Never having destroyed anything in the house, she'd always let us know when she needed to go outside. She would ride in the truck with us and watch where we were going. We often took her to our local park and walked her there, and she thoroughly seemed to enjoy chasing the ducks and turtles that would often rest on the banks of the small lake. She was never a problem, and I cannot stress enough that we loved her unconditionally.

Things rocked along for six and a half years, Blackie, of course, sharing a significant role in our lives. I even began calling her my best friend. Renee walked down the long dirt road beside our home with her twice each day. I would lie down in the evenings in front of the TV, trying to relieve my sciatica, and Blackie would come and lie down with me and place her head on my hands and just lie there. It was her way of loving me; I thought. We recently watched a documentary that said domestic dogs have two friendly genes that wild wolves or coyotes do not have. I believe it! Blackie was the best one could expect from a domestic dog.

Last year, after being with us for six and a half years, Blackie became sick one night and very lethargic. She would not eat or drink, so we knew something was wrong. She just lay on the floor and would barely move. We called our vet, and he said to have her there first thing in the morning, so we stayed up with her all night. When Renee finally got her to go outside to do her business, she crawled over into one of our numerous flower beds and lay down, and we knew what that meant. Death was what she was ready for! She knew it, but we had a tough time accepting it. She was too young, and she should have nothing wrong with her.

The next morning, we were at the vet's office when it opened. Our vet looked at her and said it did not look good, but he would run some tests and keep her through the day to see if they could get some food and drink <u>in</u> her. We said goodbye to her and left, not knowing that a little over an hour later, the vet would call us to say she did not make it. We were both heartbroken. We had learned so much from her, and she had given her love freely to us.

The vet gave us the option of getting her body buried or having her cremated, so we opted for the cremation. Three days later, the vet called back and said her cremains were ready for pickup. In addition, they returned her collar, her ID, a lock of her hair in a small see-through case, and her paw prints on a card. A year later, Blackie's picture, her box of remains, and other things are on our mantle, where they will continue to be. We really loved that dog, and she loved us as well.

Wouldn't you know it? I had to have another Boykin Spaniel! So, I called a friend of mine back home who raises them and reserved his next female Boykin. We would have to wait on the tail docking, weaning, and all her shots being up to date. When we went to pick her up, she came out like this little ball of fur that we immediately fell in love with. She was so friendly and cute, and we knew she was ours. We have had Sassy now for one year, but she will never replace Blackie. She is still learning our expectations, and we are getting accustomed to her as well. She has opened our hearts and is winning us over.

I often wonder what joy people are missing by not having a best friend dog in their lives. I will always treasure Blackie's memory, but we are now making fresh memories with our dear little Sassy. Her arrival has again brought joy to our hearts.

BUTTERFLY KISSES

My beloved daughter, Angie, approached me one fateful day, her eyes sparkling with excitement, and asked if I would be the one to perform her wedding ceremony. I gasped in surprise! First, the thought of her marrying and leaving our home felt like an insurmountable shift in the universe. Second, as any father would feel, I questioned her readiness for such a monumental step. Yet, her resolve was like a force of nature, unstoppable. Last, the emotional weight of officiating her ceremony loomed heavily over me; could I truly navigate such depths without succumbing to tears? Throughout my ministry, I had blessed over a hundred unions, yet this one felt unlike before—my precious little girl, standing before me, ready to embark on a new journey with her chosen partner. Could I rise to the occasion? Doubt lingered.

Then came her next request: "Dad, I want you to sing 'Butterfly Kisses' [a song recorded by Bob Carlisle], accompanied by the soundtrack."

How could I refuse my daughter? Little did I know the emotional strain it would impose upon me.

"Butterfly Kisses" captures the poignant evolution of a father watching his daughter bloom from a child to a woman, falling in love and venturing into life beyond her childhood home. It's a heart-wrenching melody, and now, I was to sing it at her wedding while also officiating! My heart was already in turmoil.

Renee reassured me, "You can do it, honey. I believe in you."

It was easy for her to say; she wouldn't be the one singing or leading the ceremony in front of our congregation—around a hundred beloved friends, family, and church members who had watched Angie grow.

To add to the challenge, Angie requested I don my clergy robe and stole, even in the sweltering heat of July in South Georgia! I could already envision the beads of sweat forming under that heavy robe, threatening to choke me during the ceremony.

The day of the wedding arrived, and there I stood, center stage, before the congregation. After welcoming everyone, the music began, and I sang "Butterfly Kisses." At that moment, with Angie and Heath yet to enter, I felt a fleeting calm. However, as my voice quivered near the end and I stumbled over a few lines, I wondered if I could continue, but with divine aid, I finished.

Then, the wedding party strode down the aisle, and soon it was time for my little girl to enter, adorned in a breathtaking white gown. As she approached, my emotions swelled, and I momentarily lost my composure somewhere around the third pew. A lump formed in my throat, and I knew I would need divine strength to carry on.

I navigated through the preliminary scripture readings and exhortations, but when I posed the question, "Who gives this woman to be married to this man?" I faltered!

After what felt like an eternity, I said, "Her mother and I."

In that instant, the reality hit me hard: this moment was official! Life would never be the same. No longer would she play in our backyard, sleep in her childhood room, or share nightly goodnights. She would soon move a thousand miles away to Memphis, Tennessee, beyond our protective embrace!

Thoughts raced through my mind: Did we equip her enough for this transformative moment? Had we prepared her well for the world's challenges?

I persevered through the rest of the ceremony, introducing them as "Husband and Wife." As they turned to exit down the aisle, the processional music began, and there went my little girl, hand in hand with her husband.

I recalled the feelings from my wedding as they walked away. It was a late Friday evening. I had left juvenile court early, driving my new 1971 Volkswagen Super Beetle and parking beside the small country church where we would wed. Renee, just nineteen, and I, twenty-one, exchanged vows in a quaint setting filled with love.

Mt. Olivet Church, perched on a hill, could hold around a hundred people, though only about thirty attended our ceremony. My best friend stood as my best man, while her sister was the bridesmaid. Her father walked her down the short aisle, and the ceremony, performed by my district superintendent, was short and sweet.

With no reception, we dashed from the altar into our little VW Bug, embarking on a dark journey towards Atlanta, and subsequently to our honeymoon at Lookout Mountain and Chattanooga, Tennessee. After a brief stay, we returned home to a one-bedroom parsonage connected to a grand old house across from First Methodist Church, where I served as associate pastor. Renee continued her education, while I juggled three small country churches, my juvenile court work, and night classes. We had leaped from the frying pan into the fire! Together, we would serve churches across South Georgia, raise two wonderful children, and transform our lives through God's guidance. One of those churches was the very place where I officiated Angie's wedding. Love and support filled the community.

Reflecting on our journey, we felt truly blessed. Starting with an annual income of less than $4,000 in 1972, we navigated college, groceries, and life's challenges. Our beautiful children, Angie, now a kindergarten teacher, and

Jonathan, a successful mechanical engineer in Atlanta, fill our lives with joy.

Each day has been a transformation for us, and I can see the pivotal moments that shaped who we are. While many express a desire to return to their beginnings, we are the opposite; we embrace the journey, knowing that God has transformed us every step of the way.

Last year, Renee and I discovered the most peculiar caterpillar on our lemon tree. At first glance, we mistook it for a bird dropping, but its movement revealed its true nature. We carefully placed it in a jar with leaves for sustenance and set it on our porch. Days passed, and it eventually wove a cocoon on a twig within the jar. Anticipation grew as we awaited the transformation.

One morning, I ventured out to find a magnificent giant swallowtail butterfly perched upon the twig unfurling its splendid wings. Knowing it needed freedom, I called for Renee to witness the moment as I opened the jar. That once-ugly caterpillar had metamorphosed into a breathtaking creature!

As we released the butterfly, it lingered for a moment, as if to express gratitude before soaring into the vast sky above, filling our hearts with joy. An unknown writer once said, "God changes caterpillars into butterflies, sand into pearls, and coal into diamonds. Using time and pressure, He (God) is working on you too." Life's cycle reflects the beauty of rebirth; just as the caterpillar constructs its cocoon, dies, and is reborn, so too do we experience transformation in all its glory.

These metaphors encapsulate our existence. At every juncture, we are being shaped into what God intended us to be. Countless generations before us gave us our very being, and we will pass our legacy to those who follow. A grand tapestry of humanity intricately weaves us together, our ancestors' blood flowing through us, renewed with each heartbeat. We, like butterflies, undergo constant transformation.

We marvel at the metamorphosis of the butterfly, often forgetting that those who came before us contributed to our achievements.

Naya Rivera once said of butterflies, "Butterflies can't see their wings. They cannot see how incredibly beautiful they are, but everyone else can. People are like that as well."

Romans 12:2 (KJV) reminds us, "and do not be conformed to this world, but be ye transformed by the renewing of your mind..." Many conform to worldly ways, often unaware that transformation unfolds, whether they seek it. We are all growing, maturing, and changing, even when we cannot envision our future selves.

An unknown writer aptly noted, "Just when the caterpillar thought the world was ending, he turned into a butterfly." Metamorphosis—egg, caterpillar, cocoon, butterfly—is the journey we all traverse, even when we cannot yet see the destination.

I recall a girl from my first-grade class, fragile and shy, often alone during recess while others played. As we progressed to fourth grade, she found herself beside me in class. I began sharing snacks with her, and our friendship blossomed. Soon, whispers of "Charlie has a girlfriend" echoed through our classmates.

Though she wasn't the most conventionally attractive girl, she carried a story of resilience—growing up in a dilapidated house with six siblings and an alcoholic father, often living on welfare. Yet, our bond grew, and by ninth grade, she blossomed into a stunning young woman, eventually becoming valedictorian. She pursued higher education and became an elementary teacher.

Years later, I encountered her at a Walmart checkout. I could hardly believe my eyes; that once-overlooked girl had transformed into a beautiful woman! Unsure it was her, I approached, and she recognized me instantly. We embraced and reminisced about our past. She shared her life's journey, including her marriage to a high school teacher and the joy of raising three children. I told her of my path to ministry.

With gratitude in her eyes, she said, "Without you, I would not have made it through elementary school! Your kindness made a difference."

As we parted ways, I thanked God for allowing me to contribute to her transformation. While others overlooked her, I chose friendship, and together, we discovered the beauty in each other's growth. Our encounter was a poignant reminder of how minor acts of kindness can leave an indelible mark on someone's life, just as her resilience had left a mark on mine.

As I reflect on these moments, I realize that life is a series of transformations, much like the butterfly's journey. We all have our own cocoons from which we emerge, sometimes struggling to unfurl our wings, yet always moving toward the light of our potential. We intertwine our paths with others, and every connection profoundly shapes us.

In the end, it is the love we give and receive that truly transforms us. A daughter stepping into a new life, a butterfly emerging from its chrysalis, or an old friendship rekindling reminds us that growth and change are constants in our lives. Each step forward, each moment of compassion, further beautifies the tapestry of our shared human experience.

Let's keep supporting one another in our journeys, recognizing the beauty and potential within each of us, and always cherishing the transformations that bring us closer to who we are meant to be.

THE LEGEND OF "MR. MAC"

In my quaint hometown, a legend thrived, larger than life itself, known as Daniel Lee McLaughlin, affectionately dubbed Mr. Mac by all. Today, a baseball field stands proudly in his honor—a fitting tribute indeed. Mr. Mac devoted his days to coaching baseball, guiding young boys not just in the sport but in "the game of life," as he fondly referred to it. While his coaching techniques might have been a touch lacking, his prowess as a life coach was unparalleled. He served as our city clerk during my youth.

My family, though not affluent, navigated life's challenges through the grace of God. My mother tirelessly worked two jobs to support my father, even taking on sewing and ironing for neighbors to make ends meet.

I vividly recall the day of my inaugural Little League baseball game. A few friends and I had ventured to city hall that day to inquire with Mr. Mac about the game schedule and our positions. He noticed my worn, hole-ridden tennis shoes and asked if I had new cleats for the game. I explained that my family intended to buy some, but funds were tight at the moment. Mr. Mac, well-acquainted with my family's struggles, nodded in understanding.

"Son, if you're going to be my catcher tonight, you can't take the field without proper cleats," he said before leading me to the back room of city hall, where he stored baseball gear. There, he retrieved a box and handed it to me, encouraging me to try on the shoes.

As I opened the box, I gasped in awe at the sight of a magnificent pair of black baseball shoes adorned with gleaming white stripes! It was the last box available, as most teammates had already bought their footwear days prior.

"Mr. Mac, I can't accept these shoes. I'll just wear my tennis shoes," I protested.

He gazed at me with warmth. "Son, I understand these are tough times for you and your family. I saved this one pair for someone just like you. Take them; they are yours now."

With a profound sense of gratitude, I slipped on the shoes and laced them up. *What a perfect fit!* As I walked around that room, I felt as if I were ten feet tall!

"Son, think of those shoes as a special gift for a boy I believe in. You will be a talented player and make both me and the team proud. Always remember, when you're wearing them, give it your all. And never forget, son, I believe in you. One day, you can repay this kindness to others," Mr. Mac said.

Though his words puzzled me at eight years old, I thanked him, rushing home donned in my new shoes and uniform for the game that evening. True to spirit, I played my heart out for Mr. Mac that night and continued to do so in each subsequent game! Four years later, I graduated to Pony League, where Mr. Mac remained our sole coach.

At our inaugural practice, Mr. Mac gathered the boys around him and declared, "Cravey, come here and get suited up. You are my catcher." Although there were other capable candidates, I was his chosen one.

That year, our team traversed South Georgia, winning every game and nearly every tournament we entered. Mr. Mac's unwavering enthusiasm and steadfast belief in *his* team fueled our success. We were but a mediocre team, yet Mr. Mac instilled in us the belief that we were the best! We played beyond our limits for the man who had faith in us.

Mr. Mac faced his own challenges; his vision was severely impaired, yet he never let it show. This humble man rose above his limitations, teaching us to do the same.

To every boy who passed through that Little League and Pony League program, Mr. Mac remains a living legend, and his legacy will endure forever. The field dedicated to his memory is a tribute far grander than Yankee Stadium or Atlanta-Fulton-County Stadium. Here, an old man inspired future teachers, lawyers, doctors, and even ministers! Isn't it remarkable what a new pair of baseball shoes can do for a young boy?

In nearly every city I've pastored, I've coached baseball, striving to instill in *my* boys the lessons Mr. Mac imparted over sixty years ago.

Just a few years ago, I purchased a fresh pair of Nike baseball shoes and gifted them to a little migrant Mexican boy on my Little League team, who also was my starting catcher. It felt surreal to pass on the legacy! I've done this countless times, believing that the true spirit of Mr. Mac lives on through me in some small, yet significant way.

To this day, those words of Mr. Mac echo in my heart: "Son, one day you'll have the chance to do the same for someone else."

And so, the legend of Mr. Mac continues to thrive! Mr. Mac's spirit, in every kind gesture and moment of encouragement, shapes the lives of those fortunate enough to have known him and those touched by his legacy through others. His belief in the potential of young people, regardless of their circumstances, remains a guiding light, a reminder that a simple act of generosity can ripple through time, influencing generations.

As I reflect on the impact Mr. Mac had on my life and the lives of countless others, I am filled with gratitude and a renewed commitment to carry forward his legacy. It is not just about coaching or baseball; it's about nurturing hope, fostering dreams, and believing in the inherent goodness and potential within each young soul.

May we all strive to be "Mr. Mac" to someone in need, offering not only material gifts but also the invaluable gift of belief and support. In doing so, we ensure that the legend of Mr. Mac not only survives but thrives, inspiring future generations to recognize their worth and capabilities, much like Mr. Mac did for me all those years ago.

THE NIGHT THE LIGHTS WENT OUT IN GEORGIA

Storm clouds were gathering on the horizon that afternoon. The temperature was already below freezing, so Mom had my brother, Raymond, and I gather firewood from the woodpile to burn in our potbellied heater. The power had already gone out, so we had no lights. One lone kerosene lamp would see us through the night until bedtime. It was a bone-chilling cold. Being twelve years old, I had never faced a night like this. Sure, our power had gone out many times in my brief life, but there was just something ominous about this time.

That day, the prediction had been for freezing weather with icing overnight. We lived in an old clapboard house, and the wind howled through the cracks between the boards. After Raymond and I got our arms full of wood, we immediately headed back inside and told Mama it was hailing outside. The storm then hit about an hour later at eight, so we all went to bed. I slept in the bed with my other brother, Robert. My dad had still not made it home from work, so we were worried about him, but he could usually take care of himself in most situations. He was a World War II veteran, short in stature, but as strong as an ox! We assumed he was out with his drinking friends again and would be home late.

We huddled around that stove and prepared to go to bed. Since it was so cold, we would wear our street clothes to bed to stay warm. Mama had quilted three thick blankets for our bed. My brother, Robert, and I backed up to the potbellied stove and got our bodies as warm as possible and then ran and jumped into the bed. Raymond slept in another bed in the room by himself. We curled up into a ball and tried to get comfortable and eventually fell asleep with the wind still howling outside.

At two thirty, I awakened just enough to hear a car slowly moving its way up the little dirt lane in front of the house. It did not have a muffler, so it made a loud chugging noise as it approached our house. Raymond and I got out of bed, went to the window, and looked outside. We saw the car stop in front of our house. Someone inside the car opened the back door and pushed something big onto the road. It was very dark, and we could not make out what it was. The trees were all covered in white, frozen over. It was white everywhere, and it stressed the object thrown out onto the road.

The car quickly pulled away at that point, so we ran to Mama's bedroom and woke her up. We all bundled up and went out to see what the mound on the road was, discovering it was my dad. He was lifeless and would not move. We could smell the scent of alcohol on him and saw blood, so we all three picked him up and carried him inside. Mama lit our kerosene lamp, and we then saw him in the light and panicked. I immediately thought he was dead and began crying incessantly. Mom told me to get myself together, and that Dad needed us now more than ever. The cold permeated my heart even more than the weather. What would we do without Dad? He just could not be dead!

Mama took off his shirt while I held the lamp, and she tried to revive Dad, but he never responded. His assailants stabbed him repeatedly and left him for dead, bringing him home and throwing him out. What cruel, inhumane people were they?

So, here was our dilemma. We were poor folks living on the fringes of society, without a car or anyone else to help us. Just a mother and her three boys in the dead of winter trying to decide what to do.

Mama then sent my oldest brother, Raymond, two blocks away, to Helena's only police officer. As he took off down the dirt lane, I took off behind him, running as fast as I could. He would later say I was a ghost as I ran past him to Mr. Browning's house. I banged on the front door forever, it seemed, until he finally opened the door. My voice was trembling as I told him what the dilemma was. He said he would get dressed and beat our home in a few minutes. Raymond and I then ran back home to tell Mama that help was on the way.

It seemed like an eternity before he arrived. Mama had already bathed my dad to remove the blood, and she said he had grunted a few times.

When Mr. Browning arrived and came inside, he saw my dad's condition and told Mama we had to get him in the car, and she could accompany him to the local hospital. With roads frozen over with ice, that would be a major obstacle to getting my dad the needed help. Mama told us kids to go to our neighbor's house and ask if we could stay with them. We had done this before under better conditions, so it was no problem for them to take us in.

It would be the next day before we found out what the score was. Mr. Browning had taken Mama and Dad to the local hospital, and they had refused service to him because we did not have health insurance. So, Mama and Mr. Browning had to maneuver 35 miles of the frozen highway to bring my dad to the nearest veteran's hospital. There, they had assessed my dad and said he was an incredibly lucky man. The stabbings had occurred several times, with one knife wound four inches from his heart that could have killed him. A knife cut him above his eye; several stab wounds pierced his abdomen, and he was barely alive.

Robert, Raymond, and I went back to the house the next morning and waited with anticipation for further news. We did not have a telephone in those days, so we would rely completely on Mr. Browning to come by and tell us what was happening.

The ice storm ended later that afternoon, and the trees dripped all day from the melting ice. It was still bitterly cold, and I was just as cold in my heart, for I had feared the worst. I wanted my dad home, but we were told it would be a long recovery.

Two days later, we could see Dad with a neighbor who volunteered to drive us to the hospital in Dublin. He looked terrible. I remember having to walk down two long corridors to his ward, and we could only go in two at a time. My mom took me in with her first. Dad took my hand and just looked up at me, unable to speak because he had a stab wound in his neck.

We were all traumatized for several weeks until Dad could come home. Our neighbor again volunteered to take Mom to Dublin to pick him up.

Only three years later, my dad was involved in another incident and would die from a brain hematoma following a blunt blow to his forehead. Our family suffered in those days. My mother worked at two separate jobs for us to survive, but we made it by the grace of God.

The cold is gone now, but I will never forget the night the lights went out in Georgia! That night forever changed my life.

WHAT'S MY DESTINY?

In the cherished cinematic tale, *Forrest Gump* (1994), our dear Forrest returns home to find his mother nestled in her bed, frail and weary. In this poignant moment, she reveals to him the somber truth of her impending departure. Their conversation meanders into the realm of destiny, prompting Forrest to ask, "What's my destiny, Mama?" To which she imparts the timeless wisdom, "Life is like a box of chocolates, Forrest. You never know what you're going to get."

This universal question lingers in the hearts of many: What is our destiny? Where shall our paths lead? When will we confront the inevitable?

I have often mused that knowing the exact moment of my departure from this world would be a burden I would rather not bear. Would you desire such knowledge?

Should I possess this foresight, I ponder, how would I alter my present course? Would I strive to be a beacon of goodness or seek to sow peace among the chaos? Perhaps I would dedicate my remaining days to spread love and kindness to my beloved family.

The subject of death remains a hushed whisper in the lives of most, especially regarding their own fate, yet it is an inevitability awaiting us all. As I traverse my seventy-second year, with my health in decline and blood pressure rising, the shadow of mortality feels closer than ever. I have danced with the specter of death through surgeries and procedures, and with each passing day, I glance at the obituaries, often discovering the names of those who have departed, some even younger than I. Statistically speaking, the sands of time are slipping rapidly.

While many chase fortune through lotteries or various schemes to extend their days, I hold firm in my belief in destiny. The path ahead leads us to our last moments. As the Dalai Lama wisely noted, "Remember that sometimes not getting what you want is a wonderful stroke of luck."

Years ago, a song echoed the theme of "unanswered prayers," where the singer reflects on a past love at a high school football game, expressing gratitude for the wishes that never came to fruition. The song highlights a profound truth: often, what we desire doesn't align with our destiny.

Luck is a spark many hope to ignite, with tokens like rabbit's feet carried for good fortune. Yet, as R. E. Shay aptly remarked, "Depend on the rabbit's foot if you will, but remember it did not work for the rabbit."

I resonate with the sentiment from a Verizon commercial: "I never just found my way; I made it." The journey to this moment in my life has required immense effort and unwavering faith—a testament to the power of perseverance and prayer.

So, what is *your* destiny? What have you woven into the fabric of your life to deserve a fate different from your current reality? Are you willing to change, or do you merely cast your lot and live with the results, be they joyous or sorrowful?

I often ponder the nature of my end. Will I succumb to a relentless illness that drains my vitality? Shall I endure the trials of chemotherapy, exhausting my resources for medical care? Or will I simply fade away in a quiet room, perhaps surrounded by loved ones? My wife has foreseen my demise in a fiery car crash, a fate I must admit has crossed my mind more than once. Ultimately, would we truly wish to know the day and hour of our passing? I suspect most would answer with a resounding no.

In the enchanting narrative of *Midnight in the Garden of Good and Evil*, the wise voodoo woman Minerva imparts a vital piece of advice to the young reporter: "Boy, don't commune so long with the dead you forget about the living."

If I could offer you a nugget of wisdom, dear friend, it would be just that: do not dwell on the dead or the specter of death; embrace the vibrant journey of living! Life is a fleeting tapestry woven with moments of joy, sorrow, and everything in between. It is in these moments that we truly find the essence of our existence. As we navigate the winding paths of our lives, it's important to remember that each day is a gift, an opportunity to savor the minor wonders and make meaningful connections.

Reflecting on our destiny can be an enlightening journey, prompting us to consider our values and aspirations. Are we nurturing our passions and pursuing what makes our souls sing? Are we extending kindness and compassion to those around us, leaving a positive imprint on the world? These are the questions that can guide us to live more intentionally and authentically.

Ultimately, while the mystery of destiny may remain unsolved, we have the power to shape the narrative of our lives through our choices and actions. By embracing the present and cherishing the people and experiences that enrich our journey, we can find fulfillment and purpose amidst the uncertainty.

So, as you ponder your own destiny, let it be a source of inspiration rather than worry. Allow yourself the freedom to explore, to dream, and to create a life that resonates with your true self. After all, the beauty of life lies in its unpredictability, and in our ability to find joy in the unexpected turns along the way.

THROUGH THE EYE OF A NEEDLE

Through the Eye of a Needle

My inaugural tome, *Through the Eye of a Needle,* emerged into the world in 1976, birthed by the creative hands of Brentwood Press. It draws loosely from the sacred verses of Saint Matthew's gospel, illuminating Jesus' profound discourse with a wealthy man, illustrating the challenge of entering the heavenly realm without the spirit of generosity, particularly towards the impoverished and marginalized.

Matthew 19:24 (KJV) proclaims, "And again I say unto you, it is easier for a camel to go through the eye of a needle, than for a rich man to enter into the kingdom of God." Indeed, the image of a camel navigating such a narrow passage is a vivid impossibility. For three unwavering years,

Jesus imparted lessons to his disciples on living lives of humility and service to those less fortunate.

The narrative within my book leans more towards autobiography than biblical exegesis. It chronicles the tumultuous tapestry of my childhood, the hardships my family faced, and our relentless struggle for survival. It also delves into my rebellious years, culminating in a three-month sojourn in county jail for a day of mischief that led to the breaking and entering of three establishments. Following this, a minister and a juvenile court officer guided me through probation for the next year. Many moons would pass before I embraced Christianity and dedicated my life to the service of Jesus and His church.

Once the book graced the shelves, Chicago's "Pacific Garden Missions" transformed my tale into a captivating made-for-radio drama, a thirty-minute chronicle that has resonated across national airwaves for years. Since its inception, this narrative has inspired countless souls, and I am deeply grateful that "Pacific Garden Missions" shared and dramatized my story in such a profound way.

In those early moments, I perceived my destiny as that of a mere criminal, yet God, in His infinite grace, altered my path when I surrendered my heart at eighteen. Since then, the gospel of Christ and the lives I have touched have enriched my journey immeasurably. I remain eternally grateful to the One who redeemed me, the dear friend who guided me to Christ, and the wonderful church family I have cherished for over fifty-two years. To God be the glory, now and forever!. As I reflect on the journey that began with the release of *Through the Eye of a Needle*, I am reminded of the transformative power of faith and storytelling. The process of writing and sharing my experiences was not just a cathartic endeavor for myself, but also an opportunity to connect with others who have faced similar struggles and triumphs.

Over the years, I have received countless letters and messages from readers and listeners who found solace and strength in my story. These connections have reinforced the idea that no matter how daunting our past may seem, redemption and hope are always within reach. The community that has formed around this shared narrative continues to inspire me, and I am humbled by the impact it has had on so many lives.

Looking ahead, I am filled with a renewed sense of purpose and a deep commitment to continue spreading the message of love, compassion, and redemption. Whether through writing, speaking engagements, or simply living a life of service, I am dedicated to being a beacon of light for those who find themselves in darkness, just as others once did for me.

As I embark on new projects and endeavors, I carry with me the lessons learned from my journey—a journey that began with a book and a story that, by the grace of God, continues to touch hearts and lives. May the spirit of generosity, kindness, and faith guide us all in the days to come.

Carpe Diem

From the moment we draw our first breath until our last farewell, we are journeying ever closer to the Divine. Each fleeting minute and second races by, time gently slipping through our fingers. *Carpe diem* beckons us to "seize the day" while it still holds meaning. For many elements of life elude our grasp, reminding us of its preciousness and ever-changing nature. In my youth, I was invincible, with a horizon of endless possibilities stretching before me, each plan a spark of hope.

Yet, my brother battles the shadows of dementia, struggling to navigate the labyrinth of each day. His mind, once a sharp vessel, now drifts as memories blur and thoughts twist in confusion. Both of us endured the rugged toil of farm life, and the toll on our bodies has been unforgiving. While my mental clarity remains a cherished gift, I strive to express gratitude to God each day for the ability to function and thrive.

But behold, God understands our journey toward Him and yearns for us to embrace His love and presence in our lives now.

Today's reflection arises from Matthew 10:37–38: "Whoever loves father or mother more than Me is not worthy of Me. Whoever does not take up their cross and follow Me is not worthy of Me" (KJV).

What holds the greatest importance in your life at this moment? Is it family, friends, your vocation, or the dreams that dance in your mind? These earthly ties can swiftly fade. Yet the eternal bond we cultivate with God and our communion with Him remains steadfast. When we love Him with all our hearts, we shall extend that love to others, completing the sacred cycle of connection.

In embracing this divine connection, we find the strength to face each day with courage and purpose, no matter the challenges we encounter. The love we nurture within our hearts becomes a beacon, guiding us through the darkest of times and illuminating the path for others to follow. Carrying our crosses reminds us that we are never alone.

In the quiet moments of reflection, let us ask ourselves how we can better align our lives with the teachings and love of the Divine. It is through acts of kindness, through listening with empathy, or through offering a helping hand to those in need. Each day presents an opportunity to deepen our relationship with God and to spread His love everywhere.

May we seize this day with open hearts, cherishing the time we have and using it to make a positive impact in the world. Let us live with intention, guided by faith, and driven by the desire to serve a higher purpose. In doing so, we honor the essence of *carpe diem* and fulfill our journey toward the Divine.

SPIRITUAL GROWTH IN THE BAHAMAS

In May 2001, my beloved wife and I received a heartfelt invitation to the Bahamas' second annual Spiritual Growth Conference, set to unfold at the enchanting Nassau Beach Hotel. The call was to feature me as a keynote speaker and concert artist throughout the week. My previous endeavors as a team leader for several missions to Abaco Island, where we mended homes and a local church ravaged by Hurricane Floyd, made this opportunity a delightful continuation of service. We eagerly accepted the invitation, and the warmth and camaraderie of the conference delegates embraced us.

The week's theme, "Creating New Possibilities with God," resonated deeply with me, aligning perfectly with my role as a church growth consultant within the United

Methodist Church. Together, we prayed, worshipped, and shared in joyous fellowship. Two years later, fate brought us together again in Brighton, England, during the World Methodist Conference, where they had chosen me as a delegate from Georgia. There, we rekindled our connections and celebrated the remarkable endeavors of the Bahamian Islands since my previous visit.

In a surprising twist, they even inquired if I would consider stepping into the role of bishop for the Bahamas! With their bishop's recent retirement, a void had emerged. It was a tremendous honor to be asked, yet my dear Renee chimed in with a playful warning, "There is no way you are moving to the Bahamas full time! If you feel led to take the job, I will not be going with you!" Her jest held a simple message, and I understood. Reflect on the myriad possibilities we overlook each day—God is indeed in the business of possibility.

Matthew 19:26 proclaims, "But Jesus beheld them, and said unto them, with men this is impossible; but with God all things are possible" (KJV). When we embrace the call to say yes to God, the gates of opportunity swing wide. A blessing awaits you yet remains unclaimed because of hesitation in engaging with divine potential. The possibilities of God are boundless!

Years ago, I ventured to Guyana, South America, with a mission team, and on the last day of our VBS, we extended an invitation for the youth to accept Christ as their personal Lord and Savior. To the team's astonishment, thirty-six young souls responded, committing to live for Christ! Each team member had said yes to the call to serve, and, in doing so, witnessed the remarkable transformation of those thirty-six lives.

Do you believe in the transformative power of God to work through you in ministry to the world? Open your hearts and perceive that the possibilities of God are truly endless! As we returned from the Bahamas, the memories of that vibrant community and the shared moments of spiritual growth stayed with us, inspiring us to continue our journey of faith and service. The lessons learned during the conference served as a constant reminder of the divine possibilities that await when we open ourselves to God's call.

Back home, I found myself reflecting on the many paths our lives can take when we choose to listen and act on divine guidance. The joy of witnessing lives transformed, whether on the shores of the Bahamas or in the heart of South America, reinforced my commitment to nurturing faith and fostering growth within my community.

Each encounter with a new culture, each story shared in fellowship, and each prayer whispered in unison with others added layers of depth to my understanding of faith. Spiritual growth is not a solitary journey but a collective one, where each person's story and experience enrich the tapestry of our shared faith.

As we look forward to future opportunities to serve and grow, I am reminded of the simple yet profound truth that, with God, all things are indeed possible. Whether through acts of service, moments of worship, or simply being present in the lives of others, we are all called to be vessels of divine possibility. Let us embrace this call with open hearts and eager spirits, ready to explore the endless horizons of faith together.

I Long to See You

Many moons ago, I had the honor of mentoring a young aspirant to the ministry, and I could see within him a constellation of qualities and gifts destined for the sacred halls of a church. After months of guiding him through the labyrinth of expectations in church ministry, he blossomed into an understanding of his calling, prompting me to share the news with the Board of Ordained Ministry. The church assigned him to a parish the following year.

Fast-forward a couple of years, and the junior minister reached out, his voice laden with distress. "I cannot endure this any longer! The congregation is unkind, and their words pierce my heart," he lamented. I reminded him that ministry isn't about our feelings, but about how the Divine perceives our trials and what wisdom He offers.

Later that week, we met for a heart-to-heart, sharing our burdens over a dinner table adorned with conversation. When he first called, he was on the brink of abandoning his calling, yearning to return to his previous secular life. I endeavored to ground him in the truth that ministry transcends personal tribulations; it is a divine journey. I recounted my own experiences of heartache from members in years past, many of whom transformed into cherished friends. I urged him to pray and surrender his worries to God, for He operates in wondrously mysterious ways. Miraculously, my young friend found his footing again and emerged as one of our leading ministers.

In the epistles of Paul, he penned a heartfelt letter to the church in Rome, brimming with concerns and wisdom. In Romans 1:8, he expresses, "I thank my God through Jesus Christ for you all, that your faith is spoken of throughout the whole world" (KJV). This was the essence I shared with my mentee: my constant prayers for him, my readiness to support him, and my gratitude for his dedicated service, which would soon be recognized by his congregation.

As we delve into Romans 1:11, the passage reveals Paul's longing for connection: "For I long to see you, that I may impart unto you some spiritual gift, to the end ye may be established." In our first meeting, I had imparted a spiritual gift to my young friend simply by demonstrating my love and appreciation for his endeavors.

Every soul craves encouragement. Just as Paul reached out to his fellow believers in Rome, I extended a word of support to my friend during a critical juncture in his ministry. We must uplift one another, infusing strength and faith to persevere onward.

Recently, one of my cherished mentors departed this world, succumbing to COVID-19 in the Veteran's Hospital Nursing Home in Augusta, Georgia, at the venerable age of one hundred. Two years prior, his daughter had reached out, sharing that her father wished to see me. He was still in the comfort of his home, and I journeyed to reunite with my aging companion. He welcomed me with open arms, and we reveled in the stories of our lives. At ninety-eight, he revealed that not a single day had passed in the last fifty years without him lifting me in prayer. We reminisced about children, grandchildren, and, for him, even great-great-grandchildren! What a life rich in love and purpose he had led! It was humbling to recall that I had once been his little would-be preacher. That day, my spirit renewed in the glow of such a benevolent and mighty man of God.

As I prepared to depart, we embraced once more, and he imparted a final blessing: "Charles, keep the faith as long as you live." Those words have stayed with me, echoing in my heart, and guiding my steps as I continue my journey in ministry. His unwavering faith and steadfast dedication were a testament to the power of a life lived in service to others and to God.

In reflecting on these experiences, I am reminded of the importance of community and connection in our spiritual lives. This path is not one we are meant to walk alone. We are called to support and uplift each other, to share our joys and burdens, and to inspire one another to grow in faith and love.

As I look to the future, I am filled with hope and gratitude for the mentors and mentees who have been a part of my life. Each relationship is a sacred gift, a reminder of the beautiful tapestry of connections that God weaves through our lives. And so, I strive to honor their legacy by continuing to reach out with compassion and encouragement, just as they have done for me.

May we all find the courage to be there for one another, to extend grace and understanding, and to nurture the seeds of faith within our hearts and the hearts of those around us. For in doing so, we not only strengthen our own spirits, but also create a community bound by love and guided by the light of the Divine.

Driving at Night

C. L. Doctorow wisely remarked, "Writing a novel is like driving a car at night. You can see only as far as your headlights, but you can make the entire trip that way. You just have to see two or three feet ahead of you." This profound insight illuminates the creative process: a novel begins with a singular scene, a fleeting memory, or a simple exchange. Focus on what lies just ahead, for the entirety of your tale shall unfold as you navigate the winding path of your writing.

Reflecting on my teenage years, I recall the thrill of driving at sixteen in an aging 1959 Ford. One evening, I discovered my headlights were dim, casting only a faint glow upon the road. Daylight bathed most of my journeys, but I occasionally drove after dark, facing the daunting challenge of getting home. With caution, I scanned the shadows for approaching vehicles, flickering my meager lights to signal my presence. It was a disconcerting and vulnerable experience.

The ancient sage Lao Tzu once said, "The journey of a thousand miles begins with one step." Let us not dwell on the past or fret over the future but embrace the present moment. The past has slipped through our fingers, and the future remains an elusive mirage. What truly matters is to savor the now, taking one small step at a time until we reach our destination. Indeed, I have always believed that the essence of a journey lies not in the destination itself, but in the voyage's joy we undertake. One foot in front of the other, much like the way we learned to walk as children, guides us through the pathways of life. The past is but a whisper, and the future is a distant echo. The imperative is to live fully in this moment and revel in the adventure.

In 1 Corinthians 13:12, we glimpse our human condition in relation to the divine: "For now we see through a glass, darkly; but then face to face: now I know in part; but then shall I know even as also I am known" (KJV).

I do not unravel the mysteries of God, leaving that sacred task to Him. The dark glass through which I perceive the world will grow clearer as I draw nearer to the divine. Today, I embrace the journey and eagerly expect the wonders that tomorrow may hold! Each day offers an opportunity to discover more about us and the world. Just as driving at night requires trust in the unseen road ahead, so does life ask for faith in the path we tread. Embracing uncertainty, we learn to appreciate the beauty of the unknown and the magic that comes with each new experience.

In these moments of reflection, it becomes evident that life is a series of interconnected journeys. Each choice, each moment, contributes to the tapestry of our existence. We are all travelers, navigating our own stories, each with unique challenges and triumphs. Though the path may sometimes be obscured, the light we carry within can illuminate the way forward.

So, let us cherish the present, for it is the canvas on which we paint our dreams and aspirations. With every step, every heartbeat, we inch closer to understanding the grand design of our lives. Let us move forward with courage, curiosity, and compassion, knowing that the road ahead holds endless possibilities and the potential for profound joy.

"I Just Came for the Barbeque!"

Frequently, I had the wonderful opportunity of working as a clergyperson on a Kairos weekend. Wednesday evening found forty of us in sleeping bags, camped out in the local church social hall as a team. We washed each other's feet, prayed for our team's mission to the assigned prison, and discussed the weekend's plan. We were to enter the maximum-security prison through four steel doors until we were completely inside, where we would meet the forty prisoners we would work with and pray for.

As the prisoners entered the quad on Thursday evening for a meal with us, someone matched us with our prisoner-partners for the weekend. We were not to ask what the prisoners had done to be incarcerated. They, of course, were free to share with us what they wanted us to know about them.

Kairos team members matched most of the prisoners. One remained, and since I was the only team member left, I met my partner for the weekend. He was a huge black man, approximately six-foot-eleven and 289 pounds, and a former linebacker with the Chicago Bears football team.

As we ate our meal side by side, I asked why he had signed up for the weekend Walk-to-Emmaus (Kairos). He simply looked at me and said, "I just came for the barbeque!" With other previous teams, several men prepared a barbeque meal for the prisoners, and they loved it, compared to regular prison food. I told him I didn't know if our men were planning a barbeque but assured him it would be delicious home-cooked food. He seemed pleased.

After the meal, speakers gave several talks, along with directions for the weekend. The prisoners would each sit at an assigned table with their partners throughout the weekend. Partners could share questions about the talks and answer each other's questions. There would be time for sharing during the breaks.

I would learn that my partner had been in Atlanta to play against the Atlanta Falcons one weekend and had gone with another player to the streets to purchase cocaine. The police caught him, incarcerated him, and later sentenced him to ten years in state prison. He was now in the fourth year of his imprisonment and an angry guy.

I shared the love of Christ with him as much as possible throughout the weekend, and I could tell that his heart was softening. We had barbeque on Saturday at lunchtime, so he was happy.

On Sunday morning, he approached me as we entered the quad, picking me up off the floor, and hugged me like a bear! He said, "Man, I decided last night to give my heart to Jesus! My elation and happiness for him were immense, knowing his situation and that he had six more years left on his sentence.

After we had our closing session on Sunday evening, the prisoners would return to their cells and resume their lives behind bars. Our team members would go free, back to our daily routines and lives. Two weeks later, on a Saturday, we would return to the prison for a Kairos reunion.

As guards brought the prisoners into the meeting area, my partner hugged me so tightly I couldn't breathe! He was so physically strong that I had trouble breathing until he let me go.

"Charles," he said, "I have found a whole new life behind these bars, and thank you for showing me Jesus."

We prayed together, and he gripped my hands in his like the true linebacker he had been. He was like a child with a newfound friend.

It filled both our hearts with sorrow to bid farewell at the close of our session, yet I sensed deeply that he had undergone a profound transformation. During that weekend, I encountered murderers, child offenders, extortionists, and a myriad of wrongdoers, but amidst them, I also glimpsed the radiant spirit of Jesus in the faces of those inmates who had turned their lives around. Though our paths would never cross again, I knew the boundless power and grace of a God who orchestrates the visit of ordinary souls behind the formidable walls of a maximum-security prison would forever alter their destinies to whisper messages of love.

As Francis Bacon so aptly put it, God is "the hound of heaven," eternally pursuing us through the tapestry of our lives, yearning for fellowship with each one of us. He will never abandon us nor forsake our souls.

You might wonder, "What compels you to venture into prisons to share the message of Jesus?" I humbly reference Matthew 25:36: "I was in prison, and ye came unto me" (KJV).

In truth, we are all prisoners, bound by the chains of our sins and unrighteousness. Yet Jesus loves each of us far too much to leave us in such captivity. Repent and embrace the gospel of salvation today!

Through sharing these moments of grace and redemption, we find a deeper understanding of our shared humanity. The walls that separate us become less daunting when we realize that, at our core, we all seek love, forgiveness, and a sense of belonging. The Kairos weekend was not just a journey for the prisoners, but for all of us who took part. It reminded us that no one is beyond redemption and that every life holds the potential for transformation.

As we left the prison, I carried with me the stories and faces of those I had met, knowing that their journey of faith was just beginning. It was a humbling experience that reinforced the power of compassion and the importance of reaching out to those in need, regardless of where they are in life.

This experience taught me that the simplest acts of kindness and understanding can ignite a spark of hope, even in the darkest of places. And while we may never see the full impact of our actions, we can trust that they ripple outward, touching lives in ways we may never fully comprehend.

Choosing a Life

In the evocative Spanish-American film, *The Way* (2010), Martin Sheen embarks on a poignant pilgrimage along the trail of Saint James in Spain to honor the memory of his late son, portrayed by Emilio Estevez. A haunting phrase from his son, spoken before his untimely demise on the path, lingers in Sheen's heart: "You don't choose a life, Dad. You live one." This compels him to seek clarity on the profound wisdom embedded in those words.

We cannot choose the family or lineage into which we are born. Our parents' DNA weaves our very essence, carrying with it their histories, tribulations, and lifestyles—elements we cannot choose. As Emilio told his father, we cannot control the nature of our existence.

Some emerge into the world cradled by privilege, equipped to forge a prosperous life. Others must labor tirelessly, grappling with challenges to carve out their existence. Yet, we each receive a life to embrace fully, and we should seize opportunities to improve our circumstances through steadfast dedication and hard work.

Life stands as an open door, brimming with possibilities. We hold the power to either flourish or falter. The choice lives within us. Embrace the life given to you, but do not settle for mere existence. Ascend beyond the ordinary and mundane, transforming your journey into something magnificent. You will cherish the endeavor!

Whether it's through acts of kindness, the pursuit of dreams, or the courage to face fears, each step we take on this path contributes to the tapestry of our lives. Unexpected turns and hidden treasures fill the journey, with each moment offering a lesson or an opportunity for growth. As we tread this path, let us remember that life is a canvas waiting for our unique brushstrokes. Paint it with vibrant colors of passion, compassion, and adventure. And as Martin Sheen's character discovers, it's in the living—truly living—that we find the essence of who we are and the legacy we leave behind.

DIAMONDS IN THE ROUGH

An old drunk, a battered old coffeepot, a misaligned teenager in youth detention, an out-of-wedlock, pregnant, teenaged girl... What do all these things have in common? They are all great possibilities—Diamonds in the Rough—diamonds to God our Father!

—Charles E. Cravey

Diamonds in the Rough

Surely, you have all encountered the timeless adage, "What one man sees as junk, another sees as treasure." Within every person and every circumstance lies a universe of possibilities. Ponder the plight of the old, wayward soul, lost in the haze of addiction. While family and friends may have lost hope, the Almighty never wavers!

Reflect, if you will, on the apostle Paul, once a fierce adversary of early Christians, whom a fateful event on the road to Damascus humbled, and who would persecute believers. In that moment, the Spirit of God enveloped him, igniting a profound transformation. Paul harbored immense potential, merely awaiting discovery and renewal.

Picture an old, weathered coffee pot; with diligent effort in polishing and staining, perhaps adorned with tole painting, it can bloom into a treasured artifact. It may serve as a charming ornament, a flowerpot, or countless other purposes. Indeed, it was a diamond in the rough, transformed into a splendid creation.

Consider a young teenager ensnared by a misguided crowd, facing the consequences of his choices in a detention center. There, he encounters a Bible left by the Gideons, and the Spirit's gentle whisper leads him to surrender his heart to Christ. As he immerses himself in the Scriptures, he answers the call to dedicate his life to guiding fellow youths. After years of study, he emerges from college and seminary, becoming a beacon of hope for runaways in inner cities. He, too, possesses boundless potential.

A dear friend of mine stumbled upon an old 1961 Chevrolet, hidden away in a junkyard's forgotten corner. He purchased it for a mere $50 and toiled for two years to restore its former glory, investing around $2,500. At a car show, he received an offer of over $20,000 for this diamond in the rough.

The message is simple: everything in life holds the promise of transformation, including you! You are a possibility yearning to unfold! If you humbly approach Almighty God, confessing your sins and unrighteousness, He will cleanse, restore, and breathe new life into you! With this rebirth in Christ, all things become possible!

Miners unearth a true diamond from the depths of the earth, and upon discovery, artisans meticulously cut, polish, and hone it to perfection before it adorns its rightful setting. Its value multiplies a thousandfold!

We, too, mirror this journey; when Christ finds us in our brokenness, He perfects us and grants us a new life. What an awe-inspiring God we serve! To Him belongs the glory, eternally.

I was once that diamond in the rough; perhaps you still are. Come to Christ today and let Him begin the beautiful work of perfection through His love, mercy, and grace. Embrace this journey of transformation and see how you can polish even the most overlooked facets of your life to brilliance. As you embark on this path, remember that each step is part of a greater design, leading you to a destiny filled with purpose and fulfillment.

Just as the diamond emerges from darkness to dazzle with light, so, too, can your life become a testament to the power of change and renewal. Through faith, perseverance, and the unwavering love of the Creator, you can rise above challenges and shine with a radiance that touches the lives of others.

Seek the hidden treasures within yourself and the world around you, uncovering the beauty that lies beneath the surface. With every act of kindness, every moment of reflection, and every leap of faith, you contribute to a masterpiece of grace and transformation.

Take heart, for you are not alone on this journey. The community of believers, filled with stories of redemption and hope, stands alongside you, ready to support and encourage. Together, let's celebrate the wonder of our transformation into the dazzling creations God intended us to be.

Sacrificial Love

During my childhood in Georgia, we had chickens roaming our yard. Each morning, we would gather eggs from the crib out back, which would become part of our breakfast. On special occasions like Christmas or Easter, we would choose one of the plump hens, prepare it, and serve it to our guests. One of my daily responsibilities was to ensure the chickens were well-fed and had enough water. I found joy in this task, often chatting with them as I fed them. Many of the chickens had names, and a few became special to me because they seemed to listen when I spoke. In a way, that was my first attempt at preaching!

I'll never forget one frigid winter when the crib caught fire, resulting in the loss of many hens and their chicks. A tall wire fence surrounded the crib, making it difficult to rescue them when the fire broke out. Many were too frightened and hid under feeders, nesting boxes, and anything else they could find to escape the flames. That day, I lost a significant part of my flock, and our family lost a vital source of food.

What stands out most from that day is the moment after we extinguished the fire, when we cleaned up and searched for any surviving hens. It felt like World War III in the henhouse! We had suffered a great loss.

As I was searching, I stumbled upon a charred, blackened mass because it turned out to be one of my hens. To my surprise, when it moved, six beautiful little chicks scurried out! The mother hen had sheltered her chicks under her wings, protecting them from the fire. In doing so, she sacrificed her life for their safety, allowing them to live because of her love.

This reminds me of how the scriptures portray God's love for us. He loves us with compassion, sacrifice, and unconditionality. In fact, He loved us so much that He sent His only Son, Jesus, to die on a rugged cross for our sins and those of the entire world! Christ took humanity under His wings of love, shielding us from destruction. He offers us eternal life if we place our faith in Him, believe in Him, and trust in His unwavering care. God's sacrificial love is available to everyone who calls upon Him.

A friend once posed an intriguing question: If you were on trial for serving Jesus Christ, would there be enough evidence to convict you? It's worth reflecting on! If the answer is no, perhaps it's time to reconsider how we are living our lives.

One of my favorite quotes comes from Lao Tzu, who inspires us with the idea that "A journey of a thousand miles begins with a single step." It reminds us that growth and improvement come one step at a time. Taking that first step towards a deeper faith or a more meaningful life can feel daunting, much like facing a vast, unexplored landscape. Yet, it is in those small, intentional steps that we find transformation. Just as the mother hen instinctively protected her chicks, we are called to nurture and protect the seeds of faith within us, allowing them to flourish and grow.

We can begin by seeking opportunities to serve others, showing kindness and compassion in our everyday interactions. Whether it's lending a listening ear to a friend in need or volunteering our time to help those less fortunate, these acts of love reflect the core of sacrificial living. By living with intention and purpose, we create ripples of goodness that extend far beyond our immediate circles.

In a world that often feels divided and chaotic, embracing a life of service and love can be a powerful testimony to the strength and beauty of our beliefs. By embodying the principles of compassion and grace, we become living examples of the transformative power of love, much like the mother hen who gave everything for her chicks.

May we all strive to be beacons of hope and love in our communities, drawing others towards a path of peace and understanding. As we journey forward, let us remember that each step, no matter how small, brings us closer to the heart of sacrificial love and the fulfillment of our divine purpose.

FROM SEATTLE WITH LOVE

Seattle, Washington, lies a vast 2,200 miles from Atlanta, Georgia, standing as a testament to the expanse of our great nation—a round trip would summon a staggering 4,400 miles.

Imagine embarking on such a journey in a mere two days!

Years ago, a fateful day dawned when I learned that my best friend's baby sister, battling leukemia, was nearing the end of her journey in Seattle. After undergoing a bone marrow transplant at the revered Fred Hutchinson Cancer Research Hospital, her health had waned, and she was now tethered to life support, her condition deteriorating swiftly. An infection coursed through her veins, and time was slipping away.

As my best friend conveyed this heartbreaking news, I sprang into action, making frantic calls to the Atlanta airport to secure flights for two. "Prepare yourself in thirty minutes; I'm coming to whisk you away to Seattle to be by Linda's side!" I declared with urgency.

"Cravey," he replied, as he often did, "are you completely out of your mind?"

"There's no time to waste! Pack a bag and be ready when I come to sound the horn. I've secured decent tickets, but we must reach Atlanta within three hours!" I insisted, acutely aware of the gravity that echoed through similar experiences within my community.

We departed Atlanta on a Tuesday afternoon flight, only to arrive in Seattle mere moments after Linda had taken her final breath. We were too late! The tragedy weighed heavily upon us, yet we found solace in being there for the family, offering comfort amidst their profound grief and aiding in arrangements to return her body to Georgia.

Sorrow engulfed our journey back to Georgia the following day; losing someone so cherished burdened our hearts. Knowing Linda well and having shared joyful years with her, her memory remained vibrant in our hearts. Countless souls across Georgia had rallied together, raising funds to support her through this arduous battle. In the process, the Lord weaved connections among many, strengthening the bond between my best friend and me and reminding us that even in the gravest circumstances, we could rely on each other—a truth we have always held dear.

Before our arrival in Seattle, someone informed Linda of our impending visit; she brightened momentarily, her spirits lifting as she smiled. When we entered her room, her body remained, as the family had wished for her to be with us until we arrived. Inexplicably, it felt as though she knew we were coming and departed peacefully.

Jesus taught us to love each other and help each other out. Thus, from Seattle, I send forth love—a remarkable love that holds the power to transform our world through the grace of our Lord. Love one another. In the days that followed, our hearts healed, slowly but surely. The memories of Linda's laughter and kindness became a source of comfort, a gentle reminder of the beauty she brought into our lives. We gathered with friends and family to celebrate her life, sharing stories that painted a picture of a young woman who touched so many with her warmth and generosity.

As we reflected on the journey we had undertaken, the miles we traveled were not just a physical distance, but a testament to the lengths we would go to support those we love. The experience reinforced the value of presence, of being there for one another, no matter the distance or the challenge.

In the weeks and months that followed, my best friend and I found ourselves more connected than ever. The shared experience had deepened our friendship, creating a bond fortified by shared sorrow and unwavering support. We often spoke of Linda, honoring her memory by striving to live with the same kindness and courage she embodied.

From Seattle to Georgia and everywhere in between, the journey taught us the true essence of love and friendship. It is not in the grand gestures alone but in the everyday willingness to be there, to listen, to offer a shoulder to lean on. And so, with each step forward, we carried Linda's spirit with us, guided by the love that transcends even the greatest distances.

Budget Childcare

As I drove past a daycare center adorned with the sign "Budget Childcare," a cascade of thoughts flooded my mind. The concept of a budget is familiar to me; our government wields it annually to measure expected income against expenditures for various projects and programs. Yet, when funding falls short, essential services often dwindle. The notion of "Budget Childcare" is one that eludes my understanding.

Would I truly entrust my child to such a place day after day? If one cannot afford the full fee, does that mean their child receives care of lesser quality? My mind wandered through a labyrinth of concerns regarding such an establishment.

Does this suggest that children in their care might receive only one meal instead of the customary two or three? Are they staffed by a mere two caregivers instead of the usual ten? Will the changing of a diaper become a rare occurrence, perhaps relegated to just once a day? Might this institution craft a unique budget tailored to your income? I find it hard to believe I could ever endorse their services, just as I am certain you would not; I desire nothing but the very best for my children.

Growing up, I learned the adage, "You get precisely what you pay for," a truth that has resonated with me through the years. If you seek a suit that exudes elegance, fits like a dream, and withstands the test of time, you visit a renowned tailor. Conversely, if you opt for a bargain suit from a discount store, you may find it merely adequate, soon to unravel. While we may all grapple with financial constraints, the wisdom remains: "You get what you pay for!"

In this world, some chase after fulfillment, tranquility, and happiness, yet find themselves laden with the shallow offerings it provides. They often overlook the truth that material possessions cannot quench the yearnings of their souls. Our hearts will remain restless until we discover our peace in God, who created each of us for His divine purpose. Though He ardently seeks us, longing for our companionship, how often are we too preoccupied to heed His gentle calls?

The term "budget" is a worldly construct, far removed from the divine; for God, in His infinite love, sent His finest gift, Jesus Christ, to endure a harrowing death upon a rugged cross for our sake. Truly, He made the ultimate sacrifice! In contrast, when we consider the care and nurturing of our children, the stakes are incredibly high. It's not merely about the price tag; it's about the values and priorities we hold dear. We must look beyond financial constraints and focus on the quality of love, attention, and education our children receive. Let's ensure each child has an environment that fosters their growth, encourages their curiosity, and prioritizes their well-being.

While the term "Budget Childcare" might suggest affordability, it is essential to delve deeper into what these services truly offer. Could it be possible that such centers have found innovative ways to maintain high standards without the hefty price? Perhaps these centers collaborate with local communities, employ passionate caregivers committed to making a difference, or use resources efficiently without compromising care.

Ultimately, as parents and caregivers, our role is to ensure that our choices align with the best interests of our children. By seeking and supporting childcare services that combine affordability with exceptional quality, we pave the way for a future where all children, regardless of economic background, have access to nurturing environments that foster growth and learning.

Our actions contribute to a broader understanding that cost does not always measure true value, but by the love, devotion, and dedication each child receives.

OUT OF THE MOUTH OF BABES

When our daughter, Angie, was just five years old, she brimmed with delightful surprises and remarkably profound insights. One day, as she played with an old coffee can filled with pennies and wielded her mother's wooden ladle, I chanced upon her, stirring the can with great enthusiasm. We had just returned from our morning worship, where we collected a special offering for our community's needy.

Curious about her activity, I inquired, and her response was nothing short of heartwarming: "I'm making more money for God to use!"

Isn't it wondrous to hear such beauty from the lips of a child? Might we, too, set aside our own selfish drives and ambitions, focusing instead on what we can contribute to

God's greater purpose? If we dedicate ourselves more fully to Him, He will tend to all our needs, as He has promised in His sacred word.

When we prioritize God and place Him at the forefront of all our endeavors, He, in return, will bless us and fulfill our needs. It truly is that simple. With each passing day, we can learn so much from the innocence and purity of children. Angie's simple act of stirring pennies intending to create more for a divine purpose reminds us of the potential impact of faith combined with action. Her innocent gesture is a profound reminder that even the smallest contributions, when given with a pure heart, can make a significant difference.

As adults, we often get caught up in the complexities of life, forgetting that sometimes the simplest solutions are the most powerful. Angie's example inspires us to rediscover childlike faith, letting love and a desire for selfless service guide our actions.

In a world that often emphasizes material wealth and personal success, it is refreshing to remember that true fulfillment comes not from acquiring more, but from giving more. By embodying this spirit of generosity and faith, we can inspire others and create a ripple effect of kindness and hope that reaches far beyond our immediate circles.

Let us take a moment to reflect on how we can incorporate this childlike wisdom into our daily lives, using our talents and resources to bring light and love into the world. In doing so, we align ourselves with a path of purpose and find joy giving.

In Closing

For those of you who linger in the embrace of the status quo, perched upon the fence of hesitation and shying away from the thrill of chance, an extraordinary life beckons you—if only you dare to seize it. The legendary Wayne Gretzky, that titan of ice, once proclaimed, "You miss 100 percent of the shots you don't take."

Consider the great Babe Ruth, who faced more strikeouts than home runs! It is only by embracing the unknown that you shall unearth the beauty and joy that accompany each newfound achievement and goal realized.

Without the divine presence in your life, a void of fulfillment lingers. And if you never experience love, or share your heart with another, the essence of unconditional love will remain a distant dream.

Garth Brooks' melodic offering, "The Dance," invites us to step forth and explore the new and the different. Let your spirit dance!

I have shared numerous tales within these pages of those who have twirled through their lives, like the Cart Man. Do not allow life to drift past in silence; rise and dance! Embrace the cacophony of life's music and let it guide your steps to places unknown. Each moment is a note in the symphony of your existence, and every choice you make adds to its rich tapestry. Take heart in knowing that each misstep is but a part of the grander composition, leading you ever closer to your true purpose.

As you reflect on these stories and the vibrant lives they depict, may you find inspiration to embark on your own journey of discovery and faith. Let the courage of those before you light your path, and may you author your own story with passion and conviction.

Remember, life is not merely to be observed from the sidelines but to be engaged with fully, with all its difficulties, joys, and sorrows. It is in the dance of life, with its unpredictable rhythm, that we find our true selves. So, step boldly into the dance, and let your spirit soar.

Charles E. Cravey

March 2025

I am filled with joy as I celebrate the blessed moment of my granddaughter, Meghan Marie Monahan's conversion to Christ! At the tender age of twelve, she has embraced this monumental decision, bringing a beautiful conclusion to my life's narrative! Thanks be to God! It is now my cherished honor to baptize her!

NEWSPAPERS AND MAGAZINES

Newspapers and Periodicals in Which Dr. Cravey's

Articles Have Appeared:

The Macon Telegraph

The Statesboro Herald

The Lumber City Log

The Telfair Enterprise

The Vidalia Advance

The Dublin Courier-Herald

The Wheeler County Eagle

The Fitzgerald Herald

The Sylvania Telephone

The Millen News

The Tifton Gazette

Tattnall Journal/Sentinel

Warner Robins Daily Sun

The Upper Room Devotions

Guideposts Magazine

Grice Connect (Online)

For Additional Books or Other Books by Dr. Cravey:

Https://drcharlescravey.com

www.ingramcontent.com/pod-product-compliance
Lightning Source LLC
Chambersburg PA
CBHW031430160426
43195CB00010BB/674